The Dawn Is Always New

THE LOCKERT LIBRARY OF
POETRY IN TRANSLATION

EDITORIAL ADVISER, John Frederick Nims
For other titles in the Lockert Library,
see page 203

The Dawn Is Always New

SELECTED

POETRY OF

Rocco Scotellaro

TRANSLATED BY

Ruth Feldman

AND

Brian Swann

Princeton University Press, Princeton, New Jersey

Published by Princeton University Press, Princeton, New Jersey
In the United Kingdom:
Princeton University Press, Guildford, Surrey

Library of Congress Cataloging in Publication Data will be
found on the last printed page of this book

The Lockert Library of Poetry in Translation is supported by
a bequest from Charles Lacy Lockert (1888-1974)

This book has been composed in VIP Bembo

Clothbound editions of Princeton University books
are printed on acid-free paper, and binding materials are chosen
for strength and durability

Printed in the United States of America by
Princeton University Press, Princeton, New Jersey

TABLE OF CONTENTS

x

TRANSLATORS' PREFACE

Ours was an emotional involvement with Scotellaro. We were attracted by his concrete yet evocative language, by his specific yet suggestive description of person and place. We were also moved by his passion and his modesty, as well as his courage. Some of the poems that struck home when we started to read and translate him are, in addition to a poem like "The dawn is always new" (which Carlo Levi termed "the peasant Marseillaise"), those bitter vignettes with an eerie beauty such as "To the muledriver's daughter," "A portrait all feet," and "Now that July rules."

In an unpublished essay entitled "What Remains For Poets To Do," written in 1911, Umberto Saba concluded that "it remains for poets to make poetry honest, to resist all seduction, commercial or ambitious," and to "keep oneself pure and honest in one's own eyes—this is even when the dishonest line of verse, taken by itself alone, may seem the best." Saba is talking about *coscienza*, a term which fuses conscience and consciousness. Simply opening one's eyes becomes a moral activity. Saba is just such a poet of *coscienza*. Scotellaro is another.

He is also a political poet in the fullest sense. Scotellaro is involved with the people of his town, and cares for them deeply. He gives their largely silent suffering a voice and passionate expression. His poems are open-eyed and undeceived, but they are not cynical. He does not offer "solutions" to "problems," as do politicians. Instead, he *presents*. And he suffers in the presenting, as the people he lives among suffer in their everyday existence. If the poet, because of his education, has a certain sense of alienation from his people, he turns that alienation to good account.

We have selected only the poems which we regard as the very best. But some interesting and appealing poems remain. More poems will be available to readers in the near future, when Mondadori brings out Franco Vitelli's collection of unpublished Scotellaro poems under the title *Margherite e rosolacci*. The poems in the "Additional Poems" section of this book are taken from Franco Fortini's *La poesia di Scotellaro* (Basilicata Editrice, 1974). We would like to thank Franco Fortini for making this collection available to us. All the other poems in our selection are from the one book of poems published after Scotellaro's death by Arnoldo Mondadori, with Carlo Levi as editor: *È fatto giorno*. The translators would like to express gratitude to Arnoldo Mondadori, Editore; to Ann Cornelisen, for introducing us to the poetry of Scotellaro some six or more years ago, and allowing us to use one of her photographs of Tricarico on the jacket; and to Dante Della Terza for his Introduction, as well as his clarifications and helpful suggestions. Our thanks also to Glauco Cambon for unraveling some textual tangles.

ACKNOWLEDGMENTS

Acknowledgment is made to the following magazines where some of these poems first appeared:

Antaeus, Canto, Endymion, Granite, Green House, Green River Review, Grove, Hampden-Sydney Review, International Poetry Review, Poetry Now, Sanskrit, Shantih, Small Moon, St. Andrews Review, Shore Review, Webster Review.

È fatto giorno, siamo entrati in giuoco anche noi
con i panni e le scarpe e le facce che avevamo.
Le lepri si sono ritirate e i galli cantano,
ritorna la faccia di mia madre al focolare.

Day breaks, and we too have joined the game
with the clothes, shoes, and faces that we had.
The hares have run away and the cocks crow;
my mother's face comes back to the hearth.

The Dawn Is Always New

INTRODUCTION

Something should be said, first of all, about the land where Rocco Scotellaro was born, so close to mine that I almost consider it my own. A beautiful poem written at the beginning of the century by Valéry Larbaud introduces it into European literary folklore:

> A detour of the road and the melancholy Busento
> Appears in this harsh, sterile country where far off
> On the hills spread black rotting forests,
> Cirques, vast leafless valleys
> Where, with leaden reflections, stagnant infernal waters
> Sprung from crevices in remote bituminous mountains
> That rose in deserted regions without roads,
>   without villages,
> Beside a black lake where a dark depressing winter twilight
> Seems to dwell eternally.
> Here you are, unsmiling Lucania.

Such a fascinating inferno, better known in literature, perhaps, through the animated pages of Carlo Levi's *Christ Stopped at Eboli*, had been explored by Scotellaro step by step. He could repeat by heart the names of the towns and the unknown villages from Matera to Potenza, from Potenza to the sea. The town of Tricarico, where he was born, and of which he was the first Socialist mayor from 1946 to 1950, is to us the most important point of reference for an understanding of the background and of the workings of his affections. By defining his town rather pessimistically as "the gray zone of the peasant awakening," Scotellaro reveals the difficulties with which he had to deal from the beginning of his political activity. Political structures in Scotellaro's South are shady and unclear, are gray, so to speak, and the power of what we might call blackmailing solidarity is overwhelming and unbearable: "I was like a fish-pond," Scotellaro said of himself with blunt

3

sincerity. "Both clear and dirty water flowed into me. I knew nothing about it, but among the people who voted for me were the lady president of the local Catholic Action and criminals." In such a situation, family—despite statements to the contrary—represents the only reliable protection against the adverse pressure of external events, and is the ultimate frontier of self-defense. It acts, also, as the filter through which outside influence, clean and dirty water, penetrates the zone of the individual's political survival. Rocco's father, the generous and picturesque shoemaker who dominates many of the poems of È fatto giorno, died when his son was only nineteen. Rocco's mother, Francesca Armento, a woman of great imagination and personal strength, filled the gap as best she could. With a needy family to care for, she wanted, not unnaturally, to use their one real asset, Rocco's brilliant mind, to better her family's condition. As a public figure, Scotellaro had to confront serious problems and extreme stress. He was under pressure from the people who had elected him to office: the poor peasants who daily sent the women of the family to the town hall so that they could convey to him, the mayor, their needs, their hunger for land:

> At the town-hall they shout that they want
> their piece of bread and a day's work,
> shoes, roads, everything.
> And we begin to curse together,
> mayor, swallows, women.
> ("And we begin to curse together")

His family required protection and assistance. His sister, who had children, had been left a widow when her young farmer-husband was killed at Monastir in Greece during the war ("The fair"). His mother, overcome by the family's debts, longed for her son's care and attention:

> Now you want love from me
> I cannot give.
> We are both tenants in the house,

impatient with each other;
I see you always straining
to rob me of a little affection.
You who never accustomed me to caresses.

("To a mother")

Scotellaro also had to deal with the wealthy people of the
town, those who, after the war, out of fear, had gladly dele-
gated their traditional power to the peasant's son, the red-
haired adolescent mayor whom they thought easily manage-
able because the needs of his poor family rendered him so
vulnerable.

Rocco's poetry is the center where the problems of his ex-
istence converge, the place where the different patterns of his
behavior can be discerned and analyzed. Poems dedicated to
fellow-peasants bear witness to the peasant's way of living
and dying, to his hopes and his despair, his crushing defeats
and his departures for far-away lands. Whatever may happen,
in happiness and in sorrow, the poet is with his embattled
hero. He follows him to the seaport, and waits with him for
the departing steamer; he lends him his voice to bid farewell
to life when he is struck down by violence. He accompanies
him on the nightmarish nocturnal journey that ends with the
discovery that the piece of land assigned to him by the agrar-
ian reform plan is all rocks and hardly more than pocket-
handkerchief size. He even anticipates the day on which he
will marry the peasant's daughter, the silent vestal custodian
of the hearth. But Scotellaro is most especially with him on
the day of excruciating political defeat, April 18, 1948. "We're
here alone to scream at our life," he sings with him on this
dramatic occasion. "We're alone in the storm."

And if death drowns us
no one will be with us,
in sickness and bad luck
no one will be with us.
They've barred the heavy doors to us

the ravines are flung wide open.
Again today and for two thousand years
we'll wear the same clothes.

("Black puddle: April 18")

He follows him finally to jail, February 8, 1950, when the masks have been dropped and the young mayor is expelled from the town hall because of an ill-conceived and absurd accusation of embezzlement.

Rocco's feelings toward his mother can be reduced to a famous line by Catullus: "nec tecum nec sine te vivere possum": "I can live neither with you nor without you." She was trying to impose upon him the responsibility for the household robbed of a head by the death of the father. Rocco dreams of a day when the street will sustain him and no home will be needed for his survival. In order to see this wishful thinking fulfilled, a paradoxical blasphemy that is also a supreme statement of love comes to his lips: "Muorimi, mamma mia, che ti vorrò più bene": "Please die, mother, so I may love you more" ("The grain of the sepulchre"). But in a sudden shift of mood, not atypical of his poetry, he calls upon his mother's name to seal his book È fatto giorno with a loving farewell:

Mamma tu sola sei vera
E non muori perchè sei sicura.

Mother you alone are true,
And you will not die because only you are dependable.

("Only you are true")

The more conflicting his feelings for his mother are, the more poignantly he feels the absence of his father. Rocco sees in his father the family provider he is unable to become; he is therefore brought to dramatize his father's death, and he does so by utilizing the devastating language used by Jesus when he felt abandoned by his heavenly father: "Father, Father, why hast thou forsaken me!" ("Eli Eli"). Such a desperate sense of abandonment and loneliness is a prelude to a mythical reconstruction of the father's life, from the youthful days of his traumatic but memorable experience in Paterson, New Jersey, to his pugnacious and picturesque maturity, his subdued last days and his renewed conflict with the world at the moment of his death.

> And he died—as he wanted—suddenly,
> without making peace with the world.
> When he felt the attack strike
> he groped for my mother's hand in the bed,
> he crushed it and she understood and shrank away.
> He was laid out with his face twisted,
> the rebellious words
> still in his throat.
>
> ("My father")

It has been noted that when Scotellaro reconstructed for La Terza, an important publisher, some lives capable of representing the peasant condition in the South (*Contadini del sud*) he turned to the rebellious, the restless, and the irregular, rather than the typical. (See especially the story of Michele Mulieri.) That may very well be because he was completely dominated and mesmerized by the image of his father. In a sense, he saw mirrored in the stories he was telling fragments of his father's life, the flavor and the atmosphere of its most momentous and meaningful episodes.

The answers to the problems of his life which his father's sealed lips could not give him, the signal for his departure for which he waited in vain from his possessive mother, were to be bestowed upon him by a father-figure, the economist Manlio Rossi-Doria, who told him that "a father who loves his children can only expect to see them leave" ("Economics lessons"). What could, however, appear to be a paternal blessing authorizing departure is in fact the resigned acknowledgment of the imminence of an unavoidable return. Not unlike other Southern writers (I think especially of Verga and his short

7

story *Fantasticheria*), Scotellaro calls upon witnesses to listen with him to the mournful rhythm of the village's heart. The foreign girl, *la straniera*, the girl from outside, is often a mute assenting presence, sometimes even an accomplice in wishing for the town's death. But the poet's sound and fury are reversible, and the betrayal of the city girl, the farewell to her, is accompanied by a renewed "carità del natio loco:" a rejuvenation of his love for his native land, which he seemed to have left behind forever. Unlike other Southern writers, who gladly left their destitute home towns and went out to conquer the capital (the journey to Naples of another son of a hot-blooded father comes to mind: Antonio Genovesi's journey from Castiglione to Naples), Rocco never really became accustomed to city living. As soon as he left prison, where he was held for about forty days, his friends Carlo Levi and Manlio Rossi-Doria convinced him to go elsewhere to serve the cause of the peasants, to a center of study and research, the observatory of agricultural economy in Portici, near Naples. The move was both a promotion and a demotion. The scholarly atmosphere of the observatory came into conflict with Rocco's restless activism. He missed the natural drama of his daily involvement and could not stay away from his beloved and hated home.

For some reason, Naples seems to have evoked an ancient trauma for Scotellaro. In one of his poems, "Due eroi" ("Two heroes"), the city appears as the *"machine à mourir,"* the deadly trap, for two students from Scotellaro's area. Both students were very young, both desperately attached to life: Luigi La Vista, Francesco De Sanctis' favorite pupil, killed on the barricades by the Swiss soldiers of the King of Naples in 1848, and Quinto, gunned down by the police during a political demonstration in 1951. Naples must also have represented to him the point of departure for remote lands, for that land of no return, "America scordarola," the forgetful America whose mythological presence appears from time to time in

Scotellaro's poems. However, while America is the imaginative background of his poetry, the never-never land in which his father lived for a time, Naples is something else: it is a historical presence, the hostile city, the theater of his internal conflicts. Technically, Lucania, his region, is no more than Naples' expanded back-yard, but, for Scotellaro, exile begins at the door of this region. His poetry gives us not a realistic topography, but the internal measure of space: an *"espace du dedans"* which is farther reaching and more telling than any geographic remoteness. Symbolically, although Rocco felt the first symptoms of his fatal illness during an excursion back to his own land, among his own people, he died in Portici. The image of presence and vitality is associated for him with the inferno of his home region, the roughness of the peasant's journey through life. The image of death is one with the otherness of the hostile city.

Scotellaro's poetry has an ideological component which has been carefully examined by expert critics in Italy. Carlo Levi's exaltation of the prehistorical and pre-Christian wisdom of the Lucanian peasant in his *Christ Stopped at Eboli* is well known, as is his deep influence on Rocco's political thought. However, while Levi's book is a revolutionary act, in that it is linked to the epos of the unknown, and presents to the national conscience the complete obliteration by the Italian political establishment of the peasant soul of rural Italy, it also contains poetic truths that are the product of a deformation of history, a powerful Utopia. The forgotten peasants of Italy are not confined to the South. In 1970 a writer from the Veneto, Ferdinando Camon, in a novel entitled *Il quinto stato*, presented the case of the farmer of the underdeveloped areas of the Veneto. The link between Southern history and national history has been established by great bourgeois thinkers from the South like Francesco De Sanctis, and by militant representatives of the working class like the Sardinian Antonio Gramsci. But the limits of Scotellaro's ideological position have perhaps been overemphasized. His books are the statement of a truth which is the product of an intense personal experience: we have on the one side the epos of the deprived, on the other the devastating autobiographical utterance of a Southern intellectual from a peasant family, torn between his allegiance to a reality in need of modification, and the ancestral needs of the family clan.

Scotellaro's poetic style is composite. He had great gifts, as is evidenced in his poetry, but the development of his personality was abruptly interrupted by his untimely death. In a sense, whatever he learned of his craft he learned by himself, reading books during the intervals in his political activity. As an adolescent he must have read anthologies that included such poets as Pascoli and D'Annunzio. His first poem, "Lucania," written in 1940, has echoes of Pascoli: "Il suono del campano al collo / d'un' inquieta capretta": "The sound of the bell on the neck / of a restless goat" is reminiscent of Pascoli's poem "La servetta di monte." Among the hermetic poets, he was certainly well acquainted with Quasimodo, from whom he must have learned his "stile da traduttore," a style which has a thickness, an acquired reification that is the ideal objective condition so appealing to any translator of poetry. He had carefully read Leonardo Sinisgalli, a gifted poet from his part of the country, who was also linked to the hermetic group. But although he found Sinisgalli's poetic geometry most suggestive, he repudiated his narcissism, his self-centered poetic game. In some of Scotellaro's poems an almost colloquial effect is achieved through the use of facile rhymes. In others, one finds sophisticated, even obscure poetic *raccourcis* and daring brachylogies. Occasionally the reader is confronted with the song-like rhythms of popular poetry. Scotellaro can, for instance, write:

> Tagliava con la roncella
> la suola come il pane,
> una volta fece fuori le budella
> a un figlio di cane.

With his leather-knife he cut
the sole like bread.
Once he spilled
a bastard's guts.

("My father")

Such appealing rhythm represents the least complex end of the poet's range of inspiration. A regression toward a proverbial and dialect-inspired expressive poignancy can also be detected at the beginning of poems tightly linked to local peasant situations. The opening lines of a poem dedicated to a young peasant murdered with a scythe read as follows:

Vide la morte con gli occhi e disse:
Non mi lasciate morire
con la testa sull'argine
della rotabile bianca.

He saw death staring him in the face and said:
Don't leave me to die
with my head on the side
of the white road.

("They stole you from us like an ear of corn")

The expression "vedere la morte con gli occhi" is proverbially linked in common Southern Italian discourse to a barely avoided mortal danger. The thing that is peculiar to Scotellaro's expression, and most "poetic," is that the proverbial statement has lost any metaphoric (and paradoxical) overtone and has acquired the "realistic" connotations of the dying man's hallucinations. Death is truly observed by the poet through the eyes of the mortally wounded peasant.

In this case, direct experience and autobiographical empathy express themselves through an uncomplicated scheme of cultural mediation: the critic is able to detect, without great difficulty, a natural balance between the poet's expressed intention of solidarity and the quality of the poem's imagery. There are, however, complex moments in Scotellaro's poetry in which proliferation of hypothetical meanings and the extreme intellectualization of poetic motifs create a challenge for the critic which should not be underestimated. To me, the first stanza of "Invective against solitude" (1947) forms the highest point of revelation of the hermetic, learned interference with Scotellaro's "popular" inspiration. The poet is in the hostile environment represented by Naples, surrounded by the noise of Naples' main street, the so-called Rettifilo. The noise, a constant leit-motif, helps him to annihilate the boundaries existing between the present landscape and the familiar one of Lucania. The roar of streetcars and trolley-buses becomes the roar of a torrent, the Milo, cutting with its noisy water a ravine, a laceration in the womb of the poet's home town. In a kind of oneiric transference, the poet sees a flock of "torchiari" flying, compelled by thirst, from the Norman tower from which they have been evicted.

What are the *torchiari*? At the end of the same stanza we see *"frantoiani"* (olive-grinders), whose sleep is interrupted by the horned owl's lament (*"il lamento dell'assiolo"*). *"Frantoiano"* is a typical Scotellaro neologism for *"frantoista,"* just as elsewhere, in another poem *"abigeatario"* (cattle-rustler) is an incorrect neologism for *"abigeato."* But if *torchiaro* (from *"torchio,"* wine-press) is the cliff-dwelling brother of the *frantoiano* (olive-grinder), who lives in the valley below, where do the *torchiaro*'s wings come from? There is in the poem an unbalanced parallelism between two analogous conditions: the olive-grinder, tormented by the lament of the horned owl, has a direct but dual relationship with nature, but the *torchiaro* (wine-presser) is involved in a rather complex operation. His wings are the metonymical tools of his flight toward the valley. Is Scotellaro talking of some conflict between his fellow peasants—the wine pressers—and persecuting land-owners who have expelled the *torchiari* from their rightful place? Is he establishing a vicarious analogy between the persecuted peasant evicted from the tower, and himself, who has taken momentary refuge in the city? It is very hard to say. How-

ever, no matter what obstacles to an univocal and mono-semantic interpretation of Scotellaro's "difficult" poems may exist, it is evident that poems of great power and originality can be found evenly distributed through his different thematic and stylistic zones.

I could, I suppose, be asked a question at this point concerning the degree of interest with which Scotellaro's poems are read today in Italy.

My answer would have to take into account the different facets of the complex relationship that always existed between the poet of Lucania and his reading public. For my generation, Scotellaro was, above all, a charismatic figure, the most eloquent witness of a hope we all shared for a better South, in which the needy and deprived would overcome their ancestral destitution and become a constructive part of the egalitarian future Italy dreamt of. Under pressure from unforeseen circumstances, the connotations of such a hope have been modified, and Scotellaro is no longer with us to accept the challenge of history and to enlighten the path of our lives with his generous energy.

In 1974 a book dedicated to him, *Omaggio a Scotellaro*, brought to the fore a kind of uneasiness in Scotellaro's public, prompted by what could be called his "political message." Occasional rebuttals came even from critics who were basically sympathetic to Scotellaro's poetic commitment. I believe, however, that the time has come when the cleavage between Scotellaro's opinions and our present situation is not an obstacle to an objective evaluation of his poetry. We can now base our critical appraisal of Scotellaro's works on an appreciation of the poet's daring operation with words, rather than on a content-oriented consensus.

The Scotellaro I knew was aware that life cannot truly change if words do not free themselves from eroded habits and sclerotic routines. His short-lived experience as a poet is in fact a long quest for a coherence between words he had inherited and shared with others, and images which were the

13

powerful result of his dreams, the sparks of his poetic intelligence.

His experimental restlessness is the mirror of his poetic vitality. For this reason the reader is invited to approach Scotellaro in this collection, and to take into account, above all else, the significance of his experimental legacy.

The translators' efforts should be highly commended. Ruth Feldman and Brian Swann, who have shown remarkable skill in handling the difficult poetry of Lucio Piccolo and Andrea Zanzotto, have intelligently and generously given a sophisticated English equivalent of the rhythms of a very good poet from my own land, who was also my friend. I am deeply grateful to them for their beautiful gift.

Dante Della Terza
Harvard University

FROM

Invito: Invitation

Le viole sono dei fanciulli scalzi

Sono fresche le foglie dei mandorli
i muri piovono acqua sorgiva
si scelgono la comoda riva
gli asini che trottano leggeri.
Le ragazze dagli occhi piú neri
montano altere sul carro che stride,
Marzo è un bambino in fasce che già ride.

E puoi dimenticarti dell'inverno:
che curvo sotto le salme di legna
recitavi il tuo rosario
lungo freddi chilometri
per cuocerti il volto al focolare.

Ora ritorna la zecca ai cavalli
ventila la mosca nelle stalle
e i fanciulli sono scalzi
assaltano i ciuffi delle viole.

(1948)

The violets are barefoot children

The almond leaves are cool,
the walls rain spring water;
the donkeys with lightfooted trot
choose the easy bank.
The girls with the blackest eyes
climb haughty on the creaking cart,
March is a babe in swaddling clothes, already laughing.

And you can forget winter:
you, bowed under loads of firewood,
who told your beads along many a cold mile
so you could toast your face at the hearth.

Now the tick is back on the horses,
the fly hovers in the stables
and barefoot children
assault the clumps of violets.

Le nenie

Rifanno il giuoco del girotondo
i mulinelli nella via.
Anch'io c'ero in mezzo
nei lunghi giorni di fango e di sole.
Mia madre dorme a un'ora di notte
e sogna le mie guerre nella strada
irta di unghie nere e di spade:
la strada ch'era il campo della lippa
e l'imbuto delle grida rissose
di noi monelli piú figli alle pietre.

Mamma, scacciali codesti morti
se senti la mia pena nei lamenti
dei cani che non ti danno mai pace.
E non andare a chiudermi la porta
per quanti affanni che ti ho dato
e nemmeno non ti alzare
per coprirmi di cenere la brace.
Sto in viuzze del paese a valle
dove ha sempre battuto il cuore
del mandolino nella notte.
E sto bevendo con gli zappatori,
non m'han messo il tabacco nel bicchiere,
abbiamo insieme cantato
le nenie afflitte del tempo passato
col tamburello e la zampogna.

(1947)

The dirges

The dust-devils in the street
repeat the merry-go-round's play.
I was there too in their midst
in the long days of mud and sun.
My mother sleeps at one o'clock at night
and dreams of my wars in the street
bristling with black fingernails and swords:
the street that was a playing-field for tip-cat
and funneled the quarrelsome shouts
of us urchins, more children of stones.

Mama, chase them away, those dead,
if you feel my pain in the howling
of the dogs that give you no peace.
And don't slam the door in my face
despite all the trouble I've caused you.
Don't even get up
to cover the embers with ashes for me.
I'm in the valley town's back-alleys
where the mandolin's heart
has always beaten at night.
I'm drinking with the hoers,
they haven't put tobacco in my glass.
Together we've been singing
the dirges of time past
with drum and bagpipe.

È un ritratto tutto piedi

Nella grotta in fondo al vico
stanno seduti attorno la vecchia morta,
le hanno legate le punte
delle scarpe di suola incerata.
Si vede la faccia lontana sul cuscino
il ventre gonfio di camomilla.
È un ritratto tutto piedi
da questo vano dove si balla.

(1948)

A portrait that's all feet

In the basement at the end of the lane
they are sitting around the old woman's corpse,
they've tied together the toes
of her shoes with the waxed soles.
You see her face far away on the pillow,
the belly swollen with camomile.
From this room where they're dancing,
it's a portrait all feet.

Il primo addio a Napoli

Il concertino girovago ammalia
qui, a ridosso della Duchesca,
dove giovani diciassettenni e una zoppa
hanno un cantiere di camere
in portoni sporchissimi.
Il burattinaio è un vecchio
pescatore invalido.
Ognuno solo si preoccupa
del proprio oggetto da vendere.
Ognuno fa sentire la sua voce.
Io sono meno di niente
in questa folla di stracci
presa nel gorgo dei propri affanni.
Sono un uomo di passaggio, si vede
dal cuscino che mi porta
le cose della montagna.
Il treno al binario numero otto
ci vogliono ancora molt'ore
fin che stiri le sue membra con un fischio.
Non voglio piú sentire queste rauche
carcasse dei tram.
Non voglio piú sentire di questa città,
confine dove piansero i miei padri
i loro lunghi viaggi all'oltremare.
Ritorno al bugigattolo del mio paese,
dove siamo gelosi l'un dell'altro:
sarà la notte insonne nell'attesa
delle casine imbianchite dall'alba.
Eppure è una gabbia sospesa
nel libero cielo la mia casa.

First farewell to Naples

The little strolling band enchants
here, behind the Duchesca,
where seventeen-year-old boys and a lame woman
run a business in rooms
behind filthy front doors.
The puppeteer is an old
invalid fisherman.
Everyone is concerned only with
his own merchandise.
Everyone makes his own voice heard.
I am less than nothing
in this ragged mob
caught in the maelstrom of its cares.
I am a passerby, as
the bag that holds
my mountain possessions clearly shows.

It will be many hours yet
before the train on Track 8
stirs its limbs with a whistle.
I don't want to hear these raucous
tram-carcasses any more.
I don't want to hear any more about this city,
frontier where my fathers wept
facing the long journeys overseas.
I'm going back to my dark hole of a village
where we're jealous of one another;
I'll pass a sleepless night waiting
for the little houses whitened by dawn.
And yet it is a cage suspended
in the free sky, my house.

È calda cosí la malva
The mallow is warm like this

Alla figlia del trainante

Io non so piú viverti accanto
qualcuno mi lega la voce nel petto
sei la figlia del trainante
che mi toglie il respiro sulla bocca.
Perché qui sotto di noi nella stalla
i muli si muovono nel sonno
perché tuo padre sbuffa a noi vicino
e non ancora va alto sul carro
a scacciare le stelle con la frusta.

(1947)

To the muledriver's daughter

I can no longer live beside you,
something binds my voice in my breast;
you are the muledriver's daughter
who stops the breath in my throat.
Because here below us in the stable
the mules stir in their sleep,
because your father snorts near us
and has not yet climbed up on his cart
to chase away the stars with his whip.

Per Pasqua alla promessa sposa

Il giorno, Isabella, maturerà.
Sentirai le raganelle suonare
il tempo nascosto tra le viole.
E se farai ch'io non sia solo
quando l'aria s'intinge di burrasca
e i gheppi son cacciati nella mischia
e cantano la morte del Signore
solo gli angioli deturpati, allora
con tutta l'ansia che non ti so dire
potremo insieme vivere e morire.

(1947)

To my fiancée for Easter

The day will ripen, Isabella.
You will hear the tree-frogs beating out
the time that's hidden among violets.
And if you take care I'm not left alone
when squalls darken the air,
when kestrels are tossed in the storm
and only disfigured angels sing
the Lord's death, then
with all the anxiety I can't express to you
together we shall be able to live and die.

Una dichiarazione di amore a una straniera

Non ti ho saputo dire una parola.
Senti le nostre donne
il silenzio che fanno.
Portano la toppa
dei capelli neri sulla nuca.
Hanno tutto apparecchiato
le mani sul grembo
per l'uomo che torna dalla giornata.
Silvia vuoi coricarti con me?
tanto buio s'è fatto tra di noi,
vedi, che fingono le nozze
anche i fanciulli raccolti negli spiazzi.
Vuoi sollevare per favore il sacco,
accendere il cerogeno
minuscolo sul lare,
vuoi quieta lasciarti prendere, amare?
Le nostre donne allora sono in vena
i giorni d'altalena in mezzo ai boschi.

A declaration of love to a stranger

I couldn't say a word to you.
Listen to our women,
the silence they make.
They knot their black hair
low on their necks.
Everything ready, they sit and wait,
hands resting in their laps,
for their men returning from the day's work.
Silvia will you go to bed with me?
So much darkness has grown up between us,
see—even the children gathered in the clearings
play make-believe wedding.
Will you lift the sackcloth, please,
light the tiny
candle on the shrine,
will you let yourself be taken quietly, and loved?
These are the days when our women
are in the mood for swinging deep in the woods.

L'amica di città

Il mio occhio è fatto, per guardarti,
amica, come il sole è frastagliato
dietro le quercie di prima mattina.
Hai tu la veste succinta dell'alba,
hai le labbra di carne macellata,
i seni divaricati.
Sono stato con te. Ciao, me ne vado.
Non ti scordar di me,
dei braccianti impiccioliti
nel fascio dei fanali
che scappano nei campi come lepri.

(1945)

The city sweetheart

Looking at you, love, my eye
has become notched like the sun
behind the early morning oaks.
You wear dawn's brief dress,
your lips are like fresh meat,
breasts wide apart.
I've been with you. Ciao, I'm on my way.
Do not forget me,
or the stunted field hands
caught in the lanterns' swathe,
that scatter into the fields like hares.

Sponsali

Un giorno di rigido inverno con la neve
quando le donne non amano i conversari
sedute e affaccendate attorno ai tavoli
dei loro uomini che bevono schiamazzano,
la mia vestale solitaria
del fuoco delle frasche
che attendi ch'io ti faccia
la visita di mezz'ora
ogni sera perché siamo fidanzati,
allora sarà il tempo maturo per le nozze
quando si vuole stare caldi insieme.
E fuggiremo dagl'invitati acclamanti
uno di loro girerà la chiave,
e il nostro letto sarà pronto
e noi violeremo il segreto dei bianchi confetti
posati sulla coltre dorata tra i fiori
che il giorno dopo appassiranno
e gli alberi rifiniti alla finestra
ci saranno compagni e soffriremo
la beata solitudine di sposi,
quando sarà, mia cara.
Da allora vedrò la tua faccia gialla.

(1946)

Wedding

Some stiff snowy winter day
when the women are tired of chatter
sitting, busy, around the tables
of their men who are drinking and shouting,
my solitary vestal
of the brushwood fire
waiting for me to make you
my usual half-hour evening visit
because we are engaged,
then the time will be ripe for our wedding
when people like to keep warm together.
We will escape from the cheering guests,
one of them will turn the key,
our bed will be ready
and we will violate the secret of the sugared almonds
placed on the gold coverlet among the flowers
that will fade by the next day.
The tired trees at the window
will keep us company and we will suffer
the lovely solitude of married people,
when it comes, my love.
I will see your sallow face from that day on.

Neve: Snow

A una madre

Come vuoi bene a una madre
che ti cresce nel pianto
sotto la ruota violenta della Singer
intenta ai corredi nuziali
e a rifinire le tomaie alte
delle donne contadine?

Mi sganciarono dalla tua gonna
pollastrello comprato alla sua chioccia.
Mi mandasti fuori nella strada
con la mia faccia.
La mia faccia lentigginosa ha il segno
delle tue voglie di gravida
e me la tengo in pegno.

Tu ora vorresti da me
amore che non ti so dare.
Siamo due inquilini nella casa
che ci teniamo in dispetto,
ti vedo sempre tesa
a rubarmi un po' di affetto.
Tu che a moine non mi hai avvezzato.

Una per sempre io ti ho benvoluta
quando venne l'altro figlio di papà:
nacque da un amore in fuga,
fu venduto a due sposi sterili
che facevano i contadini
in un paese vicino.
Allora alzasti per noi lo stesso letto
e ci chiamavi Rocco tutt'e due.

(1948)

To a mother

How do you love a mother
who raises you with tears
under the Singer's violent wheel
intent on trousseaux,
on making over the high uppers of shoes
for peasant women?

They pried me loose from your skirts,
a young cock bought from its broody hen.
You sent me out into the street
with just my face.
My freckles are the marks
of your whims when you were pregnant.
I hold them as a pledge.

Now you want love from me
I cannot give.
We are both tenants in the house,
uncomfortable with each other;
I see you always straining
to rob me of a little affection.
You who never accustomed me to caresses.

I started caring for you
the day papa's other son arrived.
Born of a brief fling,
he was sold to a sterile couple
who worked the land
in a neighboring village.
It was then you set up the same bed for us
and called us both Rocco.

Neve

E queste nubi sono cosí ferme
a raggiera di viola, sovrastano
gli uomini sviati sui pendii.
Se pure danno uno spillo nel sangue,
queste giornate dell'ultimo inverno
sono piú larghe di cuore nella sera.
Tu puoi sentire nella notte fonda
lievitare la neve sopra i vetri
e come si cerne fina al setello,
acceca i finestrelli delle case.
Quando il cielo porta la bufera
il piú vecchio si muove dalla seggiola
a spalare la cenere bianca:
—Non uscite, lo so io cosa accadde!
Non rasparono piú la terra
i cavalli atterriti nel valico,
il polverischio radeva sibilando,
il trainiere portava il nostro sale,
lo trovammo con la mano di pietra
spingeva ancora le ruote affogate.

(1948)

Snow

And these clouds so still
with their violet haloes, hang above
the men who have lost their way on the slopes.
Even if they sting the blood,
these days at winter's end
are larger-hearted at evening.
In the depths of night you can hear
snow rise above the panes
and as it sifts, fine, through the sieve
it blinds the windows of houses.
When the sky brings the storm
the oldest man gets up from his chair
to shovel away the white ash:
—Don't go out; I know what happened!
The terrified horses in the mountain-pass
no longer pawed the ground;
snow-grains skimmed the ground, whistling.
The muledriver was bringing us our salt;
we found him with a stone hand
still pushing the drowned wheels.

Mia sorella sposata

Me l'hanno ridotta
povera sorella,
ha la faccia tanto piccola
sulla pancia piena
che deve figliare!

Dormimmo, fa un anno,
nello stesso letto,
fissava l'attaccapanni
dov'era la sua veste.

Non mi ha nemmeno guardato,
avevamo forse vergogna,
ha chiesto una sedia alle donne,
con lei nella strada
riposava una cagna.

(1949)

My married sister

They have shrunk you for me
poor sister,
your face looks so small
above the bloated belly
that must give birth.

A year ago we slept
in the same bed,
she stared at the clothes-peg
where her dress hung.

She didn't even look at me,
maybe we were ashamed;
she asked the women for a chair.
A bitch-puppy stretched out beside her
on the street.

Mio padre

Mio padre misurava il piede destro
vendeva le scarpe fatte da maestro
nelle fiere piene di polvere.

Tagliava con la roncella
la suola come il pane,
una volta fece fuori le budella
a un figlio di cane.
Fu in una notte da non ricordare
e quando gli si chiedeva di parlare
faceva gli occhi piccoli a tutti.

A mio fratello tirava i pesi addosso
che non sapeva scrivere
i reclami delle tasse.
Aveva nelle maniche pronto
sempre un trincetto tagliente
era per la pancia dell'agente.
Mise lui la pulce nell'orecchio
al suo compagno che fu arrestato
perché un giorno disperato
mandò all'ufficio il suo banchetto
e sopra c'era un biglietto:
"Occhi di buoi
fatigate voi."

Allora non sperò piú
mio padre ciabattino
con riso fragile e senza rossore
rispondeva da un gradino

My father

My father measured the right foot,
sold expertly-made shoes
at dust-choked fairs.

With his leather-knife he cut
the sole like bread.
Once he spilled
a bastard's guts.
It happened on a night better forgotten
and when people asked him about it
he screwed his eyes up angrily.

He threw scale-weights at my brother
because he couldn't fill out
the tax forms.
He always had a sharp knife
ready up his sleeve
for the tax-collector's belly.
It was he who egged on
his crony so he got himself arrested
because one desperate day
he sent his cobbler's bench to the town-hall
with a note on it:
"All right jerk
let's see you work."

At that point he had lost hope,
my shoemaker father;
with a thin laugh and without blushing
he answered from a step:

"Sia sempre lodato" a un monsignore.
E si mise già stanco—
dal largo mantello gli uscivano gli occhi—
a posare sulla piazza, di fianco,
a difesa degli uomini che stavano a crocchi.

E morí—come volle—di subito,
senza fare la pace col mondo.
Quando avvertí l'attacco
cercò la mano di mamma nel letto,
gliela stritolava e lei capí e si ritrasse.
Era steso con la faccia stravolta,
gli era rimasta nella gola
la parola della rivolta.

Poi dissero ch'era un brav'uomo,
anche l'agente, e gli fecero frastuono.

"May He be forever praised" to a monsignore.
And already tired, with only his eyes
showing above the wide cape, he began
to station himself on the piazza, sideways,
in defense of the men standing there in knots.

And he died—as he wanted—suddenly,
without making peace with the world.
When he felt the attack strike
he groped for my mother's hand in the bed,
he crushed it and she understood and shrank away.
He was laid out with his face twisted,
the rebellious words
still in his throat.

Then they said he was a fine man,
even the tax-collector said so,
and they made a big to-do about him.

Già si sentono le mele odorare

Già si sentono le mele odorare
e puoi dormire i tuoi sonni tranquilli,
non entra farfalla
a prendere il giro attorno al lume.
Ma non ho mai sentito tante voci
insolite salirmi dalla strada
i giorni ultimi di ottobre,
il padre m'inchiodava la cassa,
la sorella mi cuciva le giubbe
ed io dovevo andarmene a studiare
nella città sconosciuta!
E mi sentivo l'anima di latte
alle dolci parole dei compagni
rimasti soli e pudichi alle porte.

Ora forse devo andarmene zitto
senza guardare indietro nessuno,
andrò a cercare un qualunque mestiere.
Qui uno straccio sventola sui fili
e le foglie mi vengono a cadere
delle mele che odorano sul capo.

(1947)

Already the apples give off their scent

Already the apples give off their scent
and you can sleep your quiet sleep,
no moth enters
to circle the lamp.
But I have never heard so many strange voices
rise to me from the street
in the last days of October;
my father nailed up my box,
my sister stitched my jackets
and I had to go away to study
in the unknown city!
And I felt my soul turn to milk
at the sweet words of my companions
who remained lonely and bashful in their doorways.

Now perhaps I should go away silently
without looking back at anyone;
I will go to seek some trade or other.
Here a rag flutters on threads
and leaves are falling
from the fragrant apples over my head.

La luna piena

La luna piena riempie i nostri letti,
camminano i muli a dolci ferri
e i cani rosicchiano gli ossi.
Si sente l'asina nel sottoscala,
i suoi brividi, il suo raschiare.
In un altro sottoscala
dorme mia madre da sessant'anni.

Full moon

The full moon fills our beds,
the mules trot on soft iron
and dogs gnaw bones.
You hear the donkey under the stairs,
its shivers, its scratching against the wall.
Under another staircase
my mother has slept for sixty years.

Canto: Song

I padri della terra se ci sentono cantare

Cantate, che cantate?
Non molestate i padri della terra.
Le tredici streghe dei paesi
si sono qui riunite nella sera.
E solo un ubriaco canta i piaceri
delle nostre disgrazie.
E solo lui può sentirsi padrone
in quest'angolo morto.
Noi sapremo di vincere la sorte
fin che dura la narcosi
del mezzo litro di vino,
se il coltello dello scongiuro
respinge la nube sui velari
nei boschi dei cerri,
se le campagne scacceranno
il vento afoso che s'è levato.

Ma i ciottoli frattanto
si affogheranno nel vallone,
i fanciulli vogliono cogliere
i bianchi confetti della grandine
sulle lastre dei balconi.
La grandine è il trofeo
dei santi maligni di giugno
e noi siamo i fanciulli
con loro alleati
tanto da sorridere
sulle terre schiaffeggiate.
Ma cosí non si piegano gli eroi

You sing: what are you singing about?
Do not disturb the fathers of the land.
The thirteen village witches
gather here in the evening.
Only a drunk sings of the pleasures
of our misfortunes.
And only he can feel like a boss
in this dead end.
We can conquer our fate
while the drug of
the wine's half-litre lasts,
if the exorcising knife
pushes the haze back onto the veils
in the forests of Spanish oaks,
if the fields drive off
the sultry wind that has come up.

Meanwhile the pebbles
will drown in the valley;
children love to pick up
the white sugared almonds of hail
from balcony tiles.
Hail is the trophy
of the malign June saints
and we are such children
with our allies
that we smile
about the pummeled earth.
But the heroes don't bend like this

con la nostra canzone scellerata.
Nei padri il broncio dura cosí a lungo.
Ci cacceranno domani dalla patria,
essi sanno aspettare
il giorno del giudizio.
Ognuno accuserà. Dirà la sua
anche la vecchia sbiancata dai lampi:
lei contro la grandine
spifferava preghiere sul grembo
dalla porta a terreno della casa.

with our wicked song.
The fathers stay angry for a long long time.
Tomorrow they'll drive us from our homeland,
they can wait
for the day of judgment.
Everyone will make his accusation. Even the old woman
blanched by lightning will have her say:
hunched over, she blurted out
prayers against hail
from the ground-floor door of the house.

FROM
Capostorno: Capostorno

Tu non ci fai dormire cuculo disperato

Tutt'intorno le montagne brune
è ricresciuto il tuo colore
settembre amico delle mie contrade.
Ti sei cacciato in mezzo a noi,
t'hanno sentito accanto le nostre donne
quando naufraghi grilli
dalle ristoppie arse del paese
si sollevano alle porte con un grido.
E c'è verghe di fichi seccati
e i pomidoro verdi sulle volte
e il sacco del grano duro, il mucchio
delle mandorle abbattute.

Tu non ci fai dormire
cuculo disperato,
col tuo richiamo:
Sí, ridaremo i passi alle trazzere,
ci metteremo alle fatiche domani
che i fiumi ritorneranno gialli
sotto i calanchi
e il vento ci turbinerà
i mantelli negli armadi.

(1947)

You will not let us sleep, desperate cuckoo

All around the brown mountains
your color has grown back,
September friend of my region.
You thrust yourself among us;
our women have heard you nearby
when castaway crickets
rise screeching to the doors
from the burnt stubble of the countryside.
There are sticks of dried figs
and green tomatoes hanging under the vaults
and the sack of wheat, the heap
of knocked-down almonds.

You will not let us sleep
desperate cuckoo,
with your call:
Yes, we will go back to the paths,
we will get down to work again tomorrow
when the streams turn yellow again
under the furrows
and the wind will swirl
the cloaks in our wardrobes.

Ti rubarono a noi come una spiga

per un giovane amico assassinato

Vide la morte con gli occhi e disse:
Non mi lasciate morire
con la testa sull'argine
della rotabile bianca.
Non passano che corriere
veloci e traini lenti
ed autocarri pieni di carbone.
Non mi lasciate con la testa
sull'argine recisa da una falce.
Non lasciatemi la notte
con una coperta sugli occhi
tra due carabinieri
che montano di guardia.
Non so chi m'ha ucciso
portatemi a casa,
i contadini come me
si ritirano in fila nelle squadre
portatemi sul letto
dov'è morta mia madre.
Lungo è aspettare l'aurora e la legge,
domani anche il gregge
fuggirà questo pascolo bagnato.
E la mia testa la vedrete, un sasso
rotolare nelle notti

They stole you from us like an ear of corn

for a young murdered friend

He saw death staring him in the face and said:
Don't leave me to die
with my head on the side
of the white road.
Nothing passes but fast
buses, slow vans,
and trucks loaded with coal.
Don't leave me beside the road,
my head lopped off by a scythe.
Don't leave me at night
with my eyes covered
between two policemen
standing guard.
I don't know who killed me.
Take me home.
Peasants like me
retreat, orderly, into their ranks.
Lay me on the bed
where my mother died.
Dawn and the law are a long time coming.
Tomorrow even the flock
will shun this soaked fodder.
You'll see my head, a stone
rolling at night

per la cinta delle macchie.
Cosí la morte ci fa nemici!
Cosí una falce taglia netto!
(Che male vi ho fatto?)
Ci faremo scambievole paura.
Nel tempo che il grano matura
al ronzare di questi rami
avremmo cantato, amici, insieme.
E il vecchio mio padre
non si taglierà le vene
a mietere da solo
i campi di avena?

through the surrounding underbrush.
This is the way death makes us enemies.
This is the way a scythe cuts clean!
(What harm did I do you?)
We will inspire fear in each other.
At the time when the wheat ripens
at the humming of these branches
we would have sung together, friends.
As for my old father:
won't he slit his veins,
left to mow
the fields of oats alone?

La fiera

per un caduto sul fronte greco

Tornano lunga fila ad alta sera
i mercanti dalla fiera.
La mamma incappucciata al focolare
s'arrossa il bianco degli occhi,
e voi bimbi aspettate
la motocarrozzetta, e tu, Angela,
il ferro piccolo da stiro
dal babbo che vi disse si partiva
alla fiera di Madonna del Monte
nella convalle tra Gròttole e Salandra.
La sua voce si è dispersa nella casa,
il suo volto l'avete incorniciato
con pochi fiori secchi sulla mensola,
il suo nome è scritto tra i caduti
di una lontana zona Monastir
dove le sue ossa sono
giorno e notte calpestate
dalle vacche d'un altro massaro come lui.

(1946)

The fair

for someone who fell on the Greek front

They file back late in the evening
the merchants from the Fair.
Her eyes redden,
the mother wrapped in a shawl at the hearth,
and you children wait
for the side-car, and you, Angela,
for the little iron
from your father who told you he was leaving
for the Fair at Madonna del Monte
in the valley between Gròttole and Salandra.
His voice is lost in the house.
You've framed his face
with a few dried flowers on the shelf;
his name's inscribed among the fallen
in a far-off place called Monastir
where his bones
are trampled day and night
by cattle of another farmer like himself.

Che si dimena tra le foglie di granturco
e la malaria lo dissangua e beve
gli dà il colore della terra maggesata
il nodoso salariato nel suo letto.
Quanti monti si caricò alle spalle
scendendo sulla verga alle marine,
ingiallivano le lettiere al sole,
la mandria turbinava l'acqua morta
dei pilacci maledetti!
Con la faccia alla soffitta
la catasta di legna cruda accanto,
le galline raschiano la terra
e pendola la coda
dell'asina sul letame,
non ha visto il fiorire del tramonto
quando i cani lamentano
e la nuvola cala sull'addiaccio.

Dové puntare i piedi alla montagna
ritornare a sentire nella morte
pungerli il granone dove nacque.

(1947)

The herd churned the dead water

The man tossing among maize-leaves—
malaria bleeds him, drinks him dry,
makes him the color of newly-turned earth,
the gnarled herdsman in his bed.
How many mountains he loaded on his shoulders
leaning on his staff, descending to the coasts;
the animals' bed-straw yellowed in the sun,
the herd churned the dead water
of the cursed mud-puddles!
Face to the low ceiling,
the heap of green wood beside him;
hens rake the ground
and the donkey's tail
hangs over the dung-heap.
He hasn't seen the twilight flower
when dogs lament
and the cloud lowers on the sheepfold.

He had to point his feet toward the mountain,
return to feel the maize among which he was born
prick him in death.

È fredda del primo verde bottiglia
che mi gioca negli occhi
la terra delle quote scarnita.
Hanno incendiato le coste dei monti
di fiaccole a olio,
scortano il cammino dei muli
tra gli specchi delle pietre e i pantani.
Sono i quotisti affamati
nella processione notturna,
ricercano con gli occhi tutto il piano
ma si hanno ognuno un ennesimo lotto.
Vengono alla terra gravida
e i solchi son numeri e segni
e sventola la giacca di velluto
su una canna
bandiera alla miseria contadina.

La scure che lampeggia ha reso
i tronchi lacerati delle quercie
ossame sparso di calcare.
Sgombra è la terra
come un cielo, senza chioma,
come un'ampia cancellata riflessa
ha l'aria del fulmine gialla.

Il primo letto tenero di grano
l'hanno razziato a notte i pastori
di stanza al di là del fosso Acquanera.
E la bestemmia si leva lontana
con la piena fervente del Bilioso

It's cold with the first bottle-green
that plays in my eyes,
the fleshless land of parcelled-out patches.
They've set the mountainsides on fire
with oil-torches;
they convoy the mule-train
among the mirrors of stones and fens.
They are the famished owners
on their night march;
they search the whole plain with their eyes
but each has a tiny plot of ground.
They come to the pregnant land;
the furrows are numbers and signs.
Their velvet jackets wave
on sticks—
banners of peasant misery.

The flashing axe has reduced
the torn trunks of oaks
to scattered limestone bones.
The earth is unencumbered
as a sky without foliage,
as a wide rail reflecting
is like yellow lightning.

At night the shepherds stationed beyond
the Acquanera ditch plundered
the first tender bed of wheat.
The cursing rises far off
with the wild floodtide of the Bilioso

fa tremare la lana sulla gregge.
E l'erba ria annacqua il cervello
alle pecore stanche ora d'inverno.
Prese dai mulinelli
rigirano intorno alla coda,
sbattono la testa a pietre e tronchi.
È come si perde l'orizzonte
ai contadini nella sera.

(1947)

making the wool quiver on the flock.
And the malign estuary grass floods the brain
of sheep, tired by now of winter.
Seized by the staggers
they chase their tails,
banging their heads against stones and tree-trunks,
the way peasants lose the horizon
in the dark of the night.

Pozzanghera nera il diciotto aprile

Carte abbaglianti e pozzanghere nere . . .
hanno pittato la luna
sui nostri muri scalcinati!
I padroni hanno dato da mangiare
quel giorno, si era tutti fratelli,
come nelle feste dei santi
abbiamo avuto il fuoco e la banda.
Ma è finita, è finita, è finita
quest'altra torrida festa
siamo qui soli a gridarci la vita
siamo noi soli nella tempesta.

E se ci affoga la morte
nessuno sarà con noi,
e col morbo e la cattiva sorte
nessuno sarà con noi.
I portoni ce li hanno sbarrati
si sono spalancati i burroni.
Oggi ancora e duemila anni
porteremo gli stessi panni.
Noi siamo rimasti la turba
la turba dei pezzenti,
quelli che strappano ai padroni
le maschere coi denti.

(1948)

Black puddle: April 18

Dazzling papers and black puddles . . .
they have painted the moon
on our peeling walls!
The bosses handed out food that day,
that day we were all brothers,
we had bonfire and band
as on holidays.
But it's over, it's over, it's over
this other steamy *festa*.
We're here alone to scream at our life.
We're alone in the storm.

And if death drowns us
no one will be with us,
in sickness and bad luck
no one will be with us.
They've barred the heavy doors to us;
the ravines are flung wide open.
Again today and for two thousand years
we'll wear the same clothes.
We're still the mob
the mob of beggars,
the ones who rip off the bosses' masks
with our teeth.

Novena per giugno

Questa è la solita strofe che ogni mattino
—dopo le morti abbondanti in ogni casa di quest'anno—
intonano gli uomini stanchi innanzi al nuovo cammino.
Già non accenna l'alba e noi siamo risospinti
per dura forza del tempo da colmare
a mettere dei gesti nell'aria ad occhi chiusi.
Ad occhi chiusi i miei paesani
partono nei campi e le corriere
turbano il silenzio che li accompagna;
i vecchi discendono sui gradini in faccia al sole,
e i merciai sulle piazze
le mani si fregano con gli oggetti svenduti,
e i fabbri pestano lo scatolame
e i reduci borbottano nelle Camere del Lavoro.
Nessuno piú prega
ma braccia infinite assiepano i campi di grano.
Solo ridà sangue ai corpi un giro rabbioso di falce
e sulle messi rivendicate all'ira della grandine
si gettano le bocche degli affamati.

(1945)

Novena for June

This is the usual verse that tired men
intone each morning as they reach the new path,
after the abundant deaths in every house this year.
No trace of dawn as yet and we are driven again
by the harsh necessity of filling time
to sketch gestures in the air, eyes closed.
Eyes closed, my fellow laborers
leave for the fields, and the buses
shake the accompanying silence;
the old men walk down the steps, faces to the sun,
and the vendors on the piazzas
rub their hands over the stuff they've sold.
The blacksmiths pound tin cans
and the veterans grumble in the Trade Unions.
No one prays any more
but countless arms crowd the wheat-fields.
Only a furious sickle-sweep puts blood back in their bodies
and famished mouths fall upon
the crops reclaimed from the hail's fury.

Sempre nuova è l'alba

The dawn is always new

Suonano mattutino

La processione è cominciata
già nella notte.
Vedo la fila dei mietitori
toccano la stella
l'unica rimasta
in cima alla strada tortuosa.
Nel mio viottolo lungo budello
i ferri dei muli sulle selci
suonano mattutino.

(1948)

Matins

The procession had already begun
during the night.
I see the row of reapers;
they touch the star,
the only one left
at the top of the crooked street.
In my lane—long gut—
the mules' iron shoes
sound matins on the paving-stones.

E ci mettiamo a maledire insieme

La stagione che alimenta
l'orgasmo tutto nostro è questa:
dai rosmarini bianchi di polvere
dai fischi delle rondini ai nidi.
Siamo nel mese innanzi alla raccolta:
brutto umore all'uomo sulla piazza
appena al variare dei venti
e le donne si muovono dalle case
capitane di vendetta.
Gridano al Comune di volere
il tozzo di pane e una giornata
e scarpe e strade e tutto.
E ci mettiamo a maledire insieme,
il sindaco e le rondini e le donne,
e il nostro urlo si fa piú forte
come quello della massaia che ha sperso
la gallina e bandisce alle strade
solitarie il suo rancore,
come quello di borea che si sente
soffiando basso alla fiamma del sole
ora cresce le molli spighe alla falce.

(1947)

And we begin to curse together

This is the season
that feeds our fever:
of rosemary white with dust,
of swallows whistling in their nests.
We're in the month before the harvest;
the men on the piazza in an ugly mood
at the winds' slightest shift
and the women leave their houses,
captains of vendetta.
At the town-hall they shout that they want
their piece of bread and a day's work,
shoes, roads, everything.
And we begin to curse together,
mayor, swallows, women.
Our shouting gets louder
like the housewife who has lost
her hen and proclaims
her anger to the empty streets,
like the north wind you feel
that blows low at the sun's flame
and now lifts the tender wheat-stalks to our sickles.

La pioggia

Mettete il vino, beviamo stasera,
è fuggito tutto il broncio dalla faccia.
Erano le foglie ritte alle robinie
lungo le siepi i rovi erano bianchi.
Le viti si aggrovigliano a levante
dove le chiama il primo vento.

Era tempo. La pioggia che si smaglia
mette le ciglia ai chicchi nella paglia,
c'è sempre un seme che germoglia da solo:
Mettete il vino, beviamo stasera.

(1946)

The rain

Bring out the wine, we'll drink tonight,
faces no longer frown.
Leaves were erect on the locust trees,
brambles white along hedges.
Vines tangle in the east
where the first wind calls them.

It was time. The dazzling rain
furs seeds in the straw;
there is always one seed that sprouts by itself.
Bring out the wine, we'll drink tonight.

Vespero

Sta l'ultimo quarto di ora
per cadere dal pendolo
nell'angolo che sarà fatto buio.
Verranno le campane dei conventi
a tuonare vicino sul mio capo.
E sono leggere e mute
hanno i volti delle statue
le femmine ai lumi.

(1947)

Evening

The last quarter of an hour is about
to fall from the pendulum
in the corner that will darken.
The convent bells will thunder
over my head.
And the women are light and silent.
They have the faces of statues
in the lamplight.

Sempre nuova è l'alba

Non gridatemi piú dentro,
non soffiatemi in cuore
i vostri fiati caldi, contadini.

Beviamoci insieme una tazza colma di vino!
che all'ilare tempo della sera
s'acquieti il nostro vento disperato.

Spuntano ai pali ancora
le teste dei briganti, e la caverna,
l'oasi verde della triste speranza,
lindo conserva un guanciale di pietra.

Ma nei sentieri non si torna indietro.
Altre ali fuggiranno
dalle paglie della cova,
perché lungo il perire dei tempi
l'alba è nuova, è nuova.

The dawn is always new

Don't yell inside me any more,
peasants, don't blow your hot breaths
into my heart.

Let's drink a cup of wine together!
That way, at the happy evening hour
our desperate wind will drop.

They still impale
outlaws' heads on stakes, and the cave,
green oasis of sad hope,
preserves a clean stone pillow.

But we don't retrace our steps on the paths.
Other wings will flee
from the nest-straw,
since along the dying of the times
the dawn is new, new.

Verde nasce: Green is born

Eli Eli

Un mezzogiorno colmo di silenzio
correvo da mio padre che potava
(dovevano fare all'amore i serpenti
sulla rotabile distesa,
soffiavano le concimaie,
la prima volta che fui solo
forse con la morte)
mi strinsi alle sue maniche come
le colombe si aggrappano agli orli.

E tante volte poi
richiamato a guardare nel vuoto
io fanciullo io solo
dato al giro puntuale della giostra.
Ed ho sputato vino
con altri bambini dalla testa grossa.
E ho saputo la rovina del pianto,
il canto del giovane Dio
e come la sera incalza anch'io:
Padre, Padre
perché tu m'hai abbandonato!

O padri quanti voi siete
fatemi ancora giocare,
non sgridatemi, non coglietemi
la torcia accesa
delle feste consumate:
è solo un baleno nel giorno lungo.

(1948)

Eli Eli

One noon brimful of silence
I ran to my father who was pruning
(the snakes must have been making love
on the stretch of highway,
the dunghills stank,
the first time perhaps
I was alone with death).
I clutched his shirtsleeves the way
doves grip edges.

So many times afterwards,
called back to stare into empty space,
I, a boy alone, absorbed in
the punctual turning of the merry-go-round,
I spat wine
with the other big-headed kids.
I knew the ruin of the lament,
the young God's song,
and as evening loomed I too cried:
Father, Father
why hast thou forsaken me!

Oh fathers—however many you may be—
let me play again,
don't yell at me, don't take away from me
the lit torch
of worn-out holidays:
it's only a lightning-flash in the long day.

Storiella del vicinato

Era cosí folla di rondini
sulle nostre teste piccine,
era facile sempre
sganciare per le scale
da una spirale di ferro
una farfalla di latta,
e si feriva a segno un'ala,
il becco, il ventre d'un rondinone.
Crescemmo a frotte in ogni vicinato
fiori di delinquenti
piedi nella guazza.
Noi morsicammo
i capezzoli delle mamme,
sono neri ora di fumo gl'incisivi.
E siamo ancora tutti vivi,
rifaremmo i giuochi ad uno ad uno,
non abbiamo piú avuto un raduno.
Oh il nostro saluto è primaverile,
è come una cangiata sottile
di sole sull'inferriata
dove in ore distinte
ci sediamo di rado.
E negl'incontri di stagione,
ci si incontra come l'acqua e il sole,
andiamo spiando nei vestiti
gli organi ingranditi
col sorriso sulla fronte.
I primi han scordato l'appello,
era un fischio d'uccello.
Ma siamo tutti presenti i compagni,

A neighborhood tale

Such a throng of swallows
over our small heads,
it was always easy
to sail a tin butterfly
from an iron ring up the steps
and—right on target—injure a wing,
the beak, the belly of a big swallow.
We grew up in swarms in every neighborhood,
flowers of delinquency,
our feet in the heavy dew.
We bit
our mothers' nipples;
those teeth are smoke-stained now.
And we're all alive still,
we'd play the old games again one by one;
we haven't gotten together.
Our greeting is springlike,
there is a kind of subtle change
of sun on the grating
where we sometimes sit
at certain hours.
And in the seasonal encounters,
we meet like sun and water,
and with smiles
we spy inside our clothes
on the organs that have grown larger.
The first ones have forgotten that the signal
was a bird whistling.
But all the old friends are present;

fin qua nessuno è caduto,
nessuno di noi è rimasto in campagna,
e nessuno è marchiato dalla fionda.
Il primo e l'ultimo fu buon soldato
dell'armata del quartiere.
Io che fui il pioniere
forse per voi mi son perduto.
Ho le carni verdi del fanciullo battuto.
Vado coi quaderni al petto
infilo le parole come insetti,
mi tengo la testa in altro mondo,
non seguo piú gli orari
dell'alba e del tramonto.
Oh le mie ossa rotte,
non sono il piú capace saltagrotte!
Dopo un lampo tra i ciliegi
contare fino a dieci
lo scoppio del tuono
io non sono piú buono.
Ogni lampo che si spegne, quel dito
che m'insegue mi ha già colpito.
Chi mi fece mettere la firma
ogni giorno che passo da riserva?
M'avete ridotto un tabernacolo.
Il capitano è sempre
il piú solo nella battaglia.
Mi affaccio di notte da questa muraglia,
tengo le fila di quei pupazzi
allegri che noi fummo.
M'avete degradato,

so far no one has fallen;
not one of us stayed in the country,
and no one is marked by the sling.
The first and the last were good soldiers
in the neighborhood army.

I, who was the pioneer,
am lost to you, perhaps.
I'm black and blue like a boy who's been thrashed.
I go round hugging my notebooks to my chest,
stringing words together like insects,
my head inhabits another world.
I no longer go by the schedules
of dawn and dusk.
Oh my broken bones;
I am no longer the best cave-jumper!
After a lightning-flash among the cherry trees
I'm no longer good
at counting to ten
before the thunder-clap.
Every flash that dies away, that finger
following has already struck me.
Who made me sign up each day
I spend in the reserves?
You have reduced me to a shrine.
The captain is always
the loneliest man in the battle.

At night I show my face at this wall,
I hold the strings
of those happy puppets we once were.
You have demoted me,

m'avete messo di guardia
e non credete che possa tradirvi
e la rondine aggressiva
davanti al mio balcone
svolta a un palmo di mano
dall'occhio del capitano.

(1948)

you have put me on guard duty;
you don't believe I can betray you.
The aggressive swallow
in front of my balcony
veers a handsbreadth away
from the captain's eye.

Verde nasce

E sono bastimenti le colline
quando il sole è sui laghi di nebbia.
Verde nasce ai pirastri lucenti,
anche la macchia è in fiore,
frasca alla montagna, erba alle marine.

O campi quanto campa quercia d'oro
cinta dai carpini molli
sulla strada vaccaglia!
I cani sentirli ansimare
e la scure del boscaiolo
ai primi caldi accesi nelle terre.

Hai rivisto i fanciulli dei tempi
spingere i cerchi di acciaio
nella corsa tra i cardi e il polverone.
Hai giocato con le còccole leggere:
tu eri a sbattere i cagnoli sulle pietre!
Hai rovistato l'uova calde dei nidi,
hai stretto nel pugno il ventre alle passere;
spezzasti i nervi alle foglie velluto
per sfilare l'iniziale di Gesú.
E la campagna aveva tanti amori,
tu eri l'amante che non sa parlare.
Perché i frutti sono a maturare
la capra ti guarda se la mungi,
ma nel cammino che ti mena lungi
dalla quercia d'oro

Green is born

And the hills are ships
when the sun is over the lakes of mist.
Green is born on the shining wild pear trees,
even the underbrush is in bloom,
branches on the mountain, grass on the coasts.

Oh fields how long this golden oak has lived
surrounded by soft hornbeams
on the cowpath!
Hear the dogs' panting
and the woodsman's axe
in the first warmth kindled in the fields.

Again you've seen the boys
rolling their steel hoops
in a race among thistles and thick dust.
You've played with the light berries:
it was you who hurled the puppies onto the stones!
You ransacked nests for their warm eggs,
squeezed sparrows' bellies in your hand;
you broke the veins in velvet leaves
to unravel Jesus's initials.
The country was so full of loves,
you were the lover who cannot speak.
Because the fruits are ready to ripen
the goat looks at you if you milk her,
but in the road that takes you far away
from the golden oak

cinta dai carpini molli
sulla strada vaccaglia,
troverai la spoglia del serpente
nelle spine ammollite
dalla bava delle vacche.

(1947)

surrounded by soft hornbeams
on the cowpath,
you will find the snake's sloughed skin
in thorns softened
by cow-slaver.

Le tombe le case . . .
cuore cuore
oltre non ti fermare.
Il fumo dei camini
nell'aria bagnata;
il passo dei nemici:
bussano alla tua porta, proprio.
Cuore cuore
oltre non ti fermare.
Le tombe le case,
novembre è venuto,
la campana: è mezzogiorno,
è lo scherzo del tempo.
I morti non possono vedere,
la mamma è cieca presso il focolare.
Cuore cuore
oltre non ti fermare.
Le tombe le case,
dirsi addio e rimandare
l'amore ad altra sera.
Come le mosche moribonde ai vetri
scorrono ai cancelli i prigionieri,
è sempre chiuso l'orizzonte.
Quanti non hanno che sperare!
cuore, non ti fermare.
Le tombe le case,
è il dieci di agosto
che abbiamo scasato.
Che fanno dove abitavamo?
Negli alberghi girano le chiavi?
I miseri, i buoni

The graves the houses . . .
heart heart
don't stop, keep beating.
Chimney smoke
in the soaked air;
the steps of enemies:
they're knocking at the door, your door.
Heart heart
don't stop, keep beating.
The graves the houses,
November is here,
the church-bell: it's noon,
time's trick.
The dead can't see,
mother is blind beside the hearth.
Heart heart
don't stop, keep beating.
The graves the houses,
saying goodbye and postponing
love to another evening.
The prisoners swarm toward the gates
like dying flies to windowpanes;
the horizon is always closed.
So many have nothing left but hope!
Heart don't stop, keep beating.
The graves the houses,
it was August 10th
when we moved to another house.
What are they doing where we used to live?
Do keys turn in hotels?
Are the poor and the good

son dannati ai traslochi?
Le donne ebree gridano sui massi
del tempio rovinato.
Quanti non hanno chi pregare!
cuore, non ti fermare.
Le tombe le case,
uomini curvi, donne aggrovigliate
si confessano alle inferriate
della Ricevitoria del lotto.
L'anima mia
è in questo respiro
che mi riempie e mi vuota.
Cosa sarà di me?
Cosa sarà di noi?
Per chi vuol camminare
dalle tombe alle case
dalle case alle tombe
grida nei cantieri
grida ai minatori
cuore, non ti fermare.

doomed to dislocation?
The Jewish women wail on the great blocks
of the ruined temple.
So many have no one to pray to!
Heart don't stop, keep beating.
The graves the houses,
stooped men, huddled women
confess at the barred windows
of the Lottery Office.
My soul
is in this breath
that fills and empties me.
What will become of me?
What will become of us?
For the man who wants to walk
from the graves to the houses
from the houses to the graves
shouting into the mineshafts
shouting to the miners
heart don't stop, keep beating.

Il cielo a bocca aperta
The open-mouthed sky

Alla fanciulla dai seni sterpigni

Non ho ancora i peli in faccia
giusti della mia età,
gli spilungoni miei compagni
mi trascinano per mano,
in un portone segnato da un globo
vogliono la tessera d'identità;
o dovevo nascere dopo.

La mia cugina non è stata mai
ardente di me,
si solleva il sottanino indifferente,
mi fa vedere
il petto bianco e le ascelle nere.

Nessuno sa dei miei tenaci amori
alla fanciulla dai seni sterpigni
allattata dall'asina, malata.
E vado accompagnando i funerali,
adulto dò la mano, piango ai suoni
dei musicanti ubriachi
per la paga dopo il cimitero.

(1946)

To the girl with the thorny breasts

I still don't have the hair on my face
I should have at my age.
My pals, those long drinks of water,
drag me by the hand.
At a big door with a globe over it
they ask for my identity card.
Oh—I should have been born later.

My girl-cousin never
burned for me.
She lifts her petticoat indifferently,
shows me white breasts and black armpits.

No one knows about my stubborn love
for the sick girl with the thorny breasts,
the girl suckled by the donkey.
And, adult, I accompany the funeral procession,
lend a hand, weep at the playing
of the musicians, drunk
on the pay they'll collect after the burial.

Il cielo a bocca aperta

A quest'ora è chiuso il vento
nel versante lungo del Basento.
E le montagne vaniscono.
E il cielo è fisso a bocca aperta.
Si vede una fanciulla nella gabbia
sopra le Murge di Pietrapertosa.
Chi sente il macigno che si sgretola
d'un tratto sulle spalle?
un rumore di serpente
il treno nella valle?
Ognuno è fedele alla sua posta.
Hanno scovato le due cagne
la lepre sul pianoro. Fugge
come lo spirito riconosciuto.

(1945)

The open-mouthed sky

At this hour the wind on the long
slope of the Basento has died down.
The mountains slip from sight,
and the sky stands still, open-mouthed.
You see a girl in the cage
above the Murge of Pietrapertosa.
Who hears the boulder that crumbles
suddenly on his shoulders?
The train in the valley no louder
than the noise of a snake?
Everyone is faithful to his post.
Two bitches have flushed
the hare on the plateau. It flees
like a ghost that is recognized.

Ancora non mi palpita una fede:
per questo mi viene la luce
e non me la sento il mattino
e so il mio giorno rapito
in un vortice inane.
Se fossi zolla!
M'avrebbe rimossa la vanga,
darei erbe e frutti
a questa stagione che sorvola.
E sono sorgente seccata
che mi scansano le greggi
ora che domina luglio.

(1943)

Now that July rules

Still no faith beats in me:
for this, light comes to me
and I feel no morning.
I know my day is seized
in an inane vortex.
If I were a clod
the hoe would have turned me over,
I would give grasses and fruits
to this season that passes over me.
I am a dried-up spring
the herds shun
now that July rules.

Andare a vedere una giovane

per una ragazza morta

In un momento ti scordasti di noi,
ti cadde dal grembo la mano
e ti compose dritta la veste nuova.
Vennero i contadini
a scoprirsi davanti a te.
Ti conobbero allora.
Presero il pugno di grano
che ti spettava il giorno delle nozze.

(1944)

Going to see a young woman

for a dead girl

In an instant you forgot us,
your hand fell from your lap
and the new dress stretched you out straight.
The peasants came
to bare their heads before you.
They knew you then.
They took the fistful of wheat
that was waiting for your wedding-day.

Margherite e rosolacci
Daisies and poppies

Attese

Le ragazze aspettano sulle porte
rosse, malariche, bianche
nelle vesti di lutto.
Cosí forse solo i carcerati
e gli studenti che contano i giorni.

Waiting

The girls wait at the red
doors, malarial, white
in their black dresses.
Perhaps only prisoners and students
count the days like them.

Giovani spose

Le nuche pettinate
delle giovani spose
del mio paese.
Nere nere nere.
Vengono nei carretti i forestieri
a prendersi la festa di vederle.

Young brides

The combed napes
of the young brides
of my village.
Black black black.
Strangers come by cart
to feast their eyes.

FROM

Il carcere: The prison

Il sole viene dopo

Sono nate le viole nei tuoi occhi
e una luce viva che prima non era,
se non tornavo quale primavera
accendeva le gemme solitarie?
Vestiti all'alba, amore, l'aria ti accoglie,
il sole viene dopo, tu sei pronta.

The sun comes later

Violets are born in your eyes
and a brilliant light that wasn't there before;
since I didn't return, what spring
kindled the lonely gems?
Get dressed at dawn, love, the air welcomes you,
the sun comes later, you are ready.

Io sono un uccello di bosco

M'hanno portato a te
i canti gemebondi della sera.
Sono il piú mansueto prigioniero
che tesse nell'ombra
le maglie con l'uncino.
Mi prese la tua luce dai cespugli,
la notte mi avrebbe sommerso:
io sono un uccello di bosco
che canta nell'aria persa.

(1950)

I am a wood bird

The evening's doleful songs
brought me to you.
I am the tamest prisoner
who crochets sweaters
in the shadow.
Your light lured me from the bushes,
night would have overwhelmed me:
I am a wood bird
singing in dark air.

Una casa dietro i cipressi del carcere

Tortora, non ti affacciare
nella tenera blusa verdemare,
i fiori sono ancora nelle foglie
e la scorza è lenta a respirare.

Carcere mio, sontuoso cancello:
mare di voci chiuse in un anello
si gonfia all'unisono per te
tortora che fai l'Ondina
tra i rami dei cipressi.
Tremula all'aria è la luce, le case . . .
e tutto non parrebbe vero,
ma tu sai tentare
col tuo becco il mio cuore.
Ma non ne sappiamo piú canzoni,
tutte le abbiamo cantate
i giorni e le nottate ai tuoi balconi.

(1950)

130

A house behind the prison cypresses

Turtledove, don't show yourself
in your delicate sea-green blouse;
the flowers are still in the leaves
and the bark is slow to breathe.

My prison, sumptuous gate:
a sea of voices closed in a ring
swells in unison for you,
turtledove, who play Undine
among the cypress boughs.
The light is a trembling of air, the houses . . .
It would all seem unreal,
yet you know how to probe
my heart with your beak.
But we know no more songs;
we've sung them all,
days and whole nights to your balconies.

La casa: The house

Casa

Come hai potuto, mia madre, durare
gli anni alla cenere del focolare,
alla finestra non ti affacci piú, mai.

E perdi le foglie, il marito, e i figli lontani,
e la fede in dio t'è caduta dalle mani,
la casa è tua ora che te ne vai.

(1951)

House

How could you endure, mother,
the years by the hearth's ashes?
You no longer show yourself at the window, never.

You lose leaves, husband, and distant sons,
and your faith in God has dropped from your hands.
Now that you're leaving, the house is yours.

C'era l'America

C'era l'America, bella, lontana
del padre mio che aveva vent'anni.
Il padre mio poté spezzarsi il cuore.
America qua, America là,
dov'è piú l'America
del padre mio?

America sarà la terra mia
col sole e la luna giganti,
aria mite, cielo celeste,
a operaio e contadino
una notte di festa.

Cosí parlavano piano:
Piroscafo che dici sí e no
sull'onda che ti tiene in mano,
voglio vedere che sorte avrò.

La Serenata apriva le porte
e notte e giorno aravo il mare
per quella terra che non l'ascoltava.
L'amico morí sparato a quella terra,
gli misero la cera in faccia,
una faccia di cera tale e quale.
Tornarono con la casa e la vigna
per un letto di gramigna
da tanto lontano.

Ora dov'è l'America nostra?
La nonna credeva all'altro mondo,
i figli leggemmo

There was America

The America of my twenty-year-old father
was beautiful, far away.
It managed to break his heart.
America here, America there,
where is it now,
my father's America?

America will be my land
with its giant sun and moon,
soft air, blue sky,
a night of feasting
for workman and peasant.

This is the way they talked softly:
Steamer that says yes and no
on the wave that holds you in its hand,
I want to see what luck's in store for me.

The Serenade opened the doors,
and night and day I ploughed the sea
toward that country which wasn't listening.
My friend died shot down in that land;
they put wax on his face,
a wax face just like his.
They came back from so far away
with a house and a vineyard
for a bed of straw.

Where is our America now?
Grandmother believed it was in another world.
We children read

le facce di cera dei padri.
Non c'è un'America nostra.
È venuto il vento,
è caduta la giostra,
è morto il vicino di casa,
che era stato a quella terra.

America qua, America là,
dov'è piú l'America
del padre mio?

(1951)

our fathers' wax faces.
For us there is no America.
The wind came,
the merry-go-round collapsed,
our next-door neighbor,
who had been in that country, died.

America here, America there,
where is it now,
my father's America?

Ho perduto la schiavitú contadina,
non mi farò piú un bicchiere contento,
ho perduto la mia libertà.
Città del lungo esilio
di silenzio in un punto bianco dei boati,
devo contare il mio tempo
con le corse dei tram,
devo disfare i miei bagagli chiusi,
regolare il mio pianto, il mio sorriso.

Addio, come addio? distese ginestre,
spalle larghe dei boschi
che rompete la faccia azzurra del cielo,
querce e cerri affratellati nel vento,
pecore attorno al pastore che dorme,
terra gialla e rapata
che sei la donna che ha partorito,
e i fratelli miei e le case dove stanno
e i sentieri dove vanno come rondini
e le donne e mamma mia,
addio, come posso dirvi addio?

Ho perduto la mia libertà:
nella fiera di luglio, calda che l'aria
non faceva passare appena le parole,
due mercanti mi hanno comprato,
uno trasse le lire e l'altro mi visitò.
Ho perduto la schiavitú contadina
dei cieli carichi, delle querce,

Journey to the city

I have lost the peasant servitude,
I will never again drink a satisfying glassful,
I have lost my liberty.
City of the long exile,
of silence in a white point of rumblings,
I have to tell time
by the trams,
I have to unpack my locked bags,
put my tears, my smile in order.

Goodbye—how can I say goodbye?—widespread broom,
you broad shoulders of woods
that break the sky's blue face,
common and Spanish oaks tangling in the wind,
sheep round the sleeping shepherd,
yellow cropped earth,
you are the woman who has given birth;
and my brothers and the houses where they live,
and the paths they climb like swallows,
and the women and my mother,
goodbye—how can I say goodbye to you?

I have lost my liberty:
during the July fair, so hot the air
could hardly carry words,
two merchants bought me,
one took out the money and the other came to see me.
I have lost the peasant servitude
of burdened skies, oaks,

della terra gialla e rapata.
La città mi apparve la notte
dopo tutto un giorno
che il treno aveva singhiozzato,
e non c'era la nostra luna
e non c'era la tavola nera della notte
e i monti s'erano persi lungo la strada.

(1950)

yellow shorn earth.
The city loomed at night
after a whole day
of the train's hiccuping.
Our moon was not to be seen,
nor night's black table,
and the mountains got lost along the way.

Tra tutte le cose che ricordo
(come le bestie, chi ha la forza
chi lo stagno del piscio e chi una fontana:
io anche sono un muletto, scelto nelle fiere
che ha avuto già tre padroni)
quella che fra tutte piú ricordo
e vive è un pezzo di stradetta
vicino a casa mia. Aveva ed ha
sempre una coperta bianca di sole
che viene da mezzogiorno: le case
davanti sono basse e scendono a valle.
Qui portavano in seggiola il vecchio garibaldino
novantenne.

Un garibaldino novantenne era
quel vecchio bue che pigliava il sole
a Fuori Porta Monte.
Gli andavo attorno come al monumento;
il grande corpo di una statua di neve
e carboni per occhi aveva.
Una volta e due
—come si fa per capire
il cenno piú vero
di un animale che capisce—
gli mettevo avanti il sussidiario
ed il ritratto del Generale
che egli non vide veramente mai.

Veniva una nipote a dargli
il pane cotto col cucchiaio,
ad aprirgli le labbra inerti di bronzo.
Mi nascosi, per giocare a moscacieca,

The ninety-year-old Garibaldino

Of all the things I remember
(like the animals: which one is the strongest,
which makes the pool of urine and which the fountain;
I too am a young mule, chosen at the fair,
that has already had three masters)
the thing I remember best
and most vividly is a stretch of lane
next to my house. It had and still has, always,
a white blanket of sun that comes
from the south. The house-fronts opposite
are low, their backs slope steeply
down to the valley.
Here they used to carry the ninety-year-old
Garibaldino on a kitchen-chair.

A ninety-year-old Garibaldino was
that old ox soaking up the sun
at Fuori Porta Monte.
I hung around him the way you hang around a monument;
he had a snowman's big body
with bits of coal for eyes.
Once, twice—
as you do to understand the clearest sign
from an animal that understands—
I held my history book up to him
and the picture of the General
he never actually saw.

A niece used to come and feed him
pap with a spoon,
opening his motionless bronze lips.
I hid under his heavy wool cloak

sotto il suo pesante mantello di lana:
èra piú caldo lui del bue nella stalla,
era piú freddo lui della statua di neve.
Calato il sole, quattro uomini
lo calavano nella casa.

(1952)

to play hide and seek.
He was warmer than an ox in the stable,
colder than a snowman.
When the sun set, four men
lowered him into the house.

Quaderno a cancelli
Checkered notebook

Cena

Voglio aria la sera e consumazione
di vino e castagne in compagnia
perché ognuno conta una storia
e insieme viene l'armonia.

Lo scarparo è stato tutto il santo giorno in casa
fino a che si è fatto scuro e si è cavato il senale,
con quello ha coperto il bancarello e i ferri
e ha detto a moglie e figli: Io esco, andatevi a coricare.
Il fabbricatore viene direttamente dalla casa che fabbrica
con le lenticchie di calce azzeccate sotto l'occhio.
Il sarto anche lui con un filo e l'impiegato
con l'inchiostro sciolto alla punta di due dita.
I contadini sono piú di uno
con succhi di stalla sul collo,
Ed io ho sbattuto il libro già ingoiato dall'ombra,
e ho detto ad alta voce che questo non è vita.
Ci siamo allora azzuffati alla morra,
la moglie e la figlia del falegname,
dove stiamo bevendo, girano attorno alla tavola
e dicono che siamo proprio bambini.
Abbiamo cacciato i tozzi di pane di tasca
e chi olive, chi una noce, chi la cipolla e il peperone;
l'impiegato ha diviso la frittata incartata
in un foglio di ufficio, e abbiamo bevuto.

Amore, amore veniva da cantarlo
tutta la santa notte in compagnia.
La moglie e la figlia del falegname
si sono ritirate dicendo:
Questi fanno far giorno.

(1952)

Supper

Evenings I feel the need of air
and sharing wine and chestnuts,
because everybody tells a story
and being together makes for harmony.

The shoemaker was home all day long
till it got dark and he took off his apron,
used it to cover his bench and tools
and told his wife and children: I'm going out. Go to bed.
The builder comes straight from the house he's putting up,
with plaster freckles sprinkled under his eyes.
The tailor too with a piece of thread, and the clerk
with two ink-stained fingertips.
There is more than one peasant
with his neck stained from the stable.
I have flung down the book already swallowed up by shadow
and announced that this is no life at all.
Then we had a really hot game of *morra*.
The wife and daughter of the carpenter,
in whose house we're drinking, hang around the table
saying we're just big kids.
We fished hunks of bread out of our pockets:
someone brought olives, somebody else nuts; another,
                                    onions and peppers;
the clerk divided up his omelette wrapped
in a sheet of official stationery, and we had plenty to drink.

We felt like singing about love
the whole damn night with our friends.
The carpenter's wife and daughter
went off to bed, saying:
This bunch is going to be here till morning.

Lezioni di economia

Ti ho chiesto un giorno chi mise
le sentinelle di abeti
visti alle Dolomiti.
Ti ho chiesto tante altre cose
del cisto, del mirto,
dell'inula viscosa,
nomi senza economia.
Mi hai risposto tra l'altro,
che un padre che ama i figli
può solo vederli andar via.

(1952)

Economics lessons

I once asked you who planted
the sentinel firs
I'd seen in the Dolomites.
I asked you so many other things
about the rock-rose, the myrtle,
the stickly inula,
extravagant names.
You answered among other things
that a father who loves his children
can only expect to see them leave.

I versi e la tagliola

Con la neve si para la tagliola
e si aspettano i gridi dei fringuelli.
La maestra ai bimbi della scuola
legge un verso d'amore per gli uccelli.
Mi piacevano i versi e la tagliola.

(1952)

The poem and the snare

With the snow they are readying the snare
and waiting for the squeaking of the chaffinches.
The teacher reads the schoolchildren
a love poem for the birds.
I liked both poem and snare.

America

Mia madre, la porto in tasca la lettera,
mio padre l'ha trovato intero, dice,
nella bara dopo dieci anni,
e non è entrato nella cassetta
fatta per averlo in cenere;
altre cinquantamila lire,
se il cugino non sfondava il tetto
della sua cappella per porlo lí,
come lo spuntone di una trave,
dopo tre giornate di fatica offerta
perché lui spera che io lo faccia partire
in America, dove ha figli e moglie,
e lui, già cittadino, non lo vogliono.

(1952)

America

I carry my mother's letter in my pocket:
it says she found my father intact
in his coffin after ten years;
he didn't fit into the box
made to hold his ashes.
Another fifty thousand lire,
if my cousin hadn't broken through the roof
of his chapel to lay him there,
like a beam-end,
after the three days of work he volunteered,
hoping I'd help him
get to America, where he has children and a wife
and isn't wanted, though he's already a citizen.

Salmo alla casa e agli emigranti

Inchinati alla terra, alla piccola porta mangiata della casa,
noi siamo i figli e la porta è carica di altri sudori,
e la terra, la nostra porzione, puzza e odora.
Mi uccidono, mi arrestano, morirò di fame, affogato
perché vento e polvere, sotto il filo della porta, ardono la gola;
nessuna altra donna mi amerà, scoppierà la guerra,
cadrà la casa, morirà mamma e perderò gli amici.
Il paese mio si va spopolando, imbarcano senza canzoni
con i nuovi corredi di camicie e mutande i miei paesani.
Che vanno a pigliare l'anello? Come nel giuoco,
sui muli bardati di coperte, e con le aste di ferro uncinate,
al filo teso sulla rotabile, nel giorno di San Pancrazio?
Ve ne andate anche voi, padri della terra, e lasciate
il filo della porta piú nero del nero fumo.
Quale spiraglio ai figli che avete fatto
quando la sera si ritireranno?

(1952)

Psalm to the house and the emigrants

Bowed to the earth, at the small worn house-door,
we are the sons. The door is soaked with other sweat,
and the land, our portion, stinks and smells.
Let them kill me, let them arrest me. I'll die of hunger, stifled
because under the door's edge wind and dust burn the throat;
no other woman will love me, war will break out,
the house will collapse, mama will die and I'll lose my friends.
My town is being deserted; they go aboard with no songs,
with new outfits of shirts and underpants, my fellow townsmen.
Will they be able to grab the gold ring the way men do
from the wire stretched across the road on San Pancrazio's Day,
astride mules saddled with blankets, using hooked iron poles?
You are leaving too, fathers of the land, leaving
the door-edge blacker than black smoke.
What gleam of hope for the children you've sired
when they go to bed in the evening?

Domenica

La città si è riunita oggi nelle chiese e nei teatri
a battere le mani. Solo i poveri e gli amanti poveri
trovano la casa sotto il portone durante la pioggia.
Ma i poveri non ci interessano oggi.
Le ragazze che rimangono in casa accanto alle madri vecchie
da custodire perché cadono dal letto.
I ragazzi che sanno l'illusione della strada e leggono i libri dietro i
vetri.
Le puttane che pure il giorno di Natale e di Pasqua
salgono le scale tirandosi le code di seta, e lavano i membri.
E tutti gli uomini e le donne, i giovani e i vecchi
che non se la sentono oggi di battere le mani.

(1952)

Sunday

The city has gathered today in churches and theatres
to clap hands. Only poor people and poor lovers
find the house under the big portal during the rain.
But the poor don't interest us today:
young girls who stay home beside old mothers
who need watching because they fall out of bed;
boys who know the street's illusion and read books
                              behind windowpanes;
whores who even on Easter and Christmas Day
climb stairs dragging silk trains behind them, and wash their
                              clients' genitals,
and all the men and women, young and old,
who feel no urge to clap hands today.

Padre mio

Padre mio che sei nel fuoco,
che brulica al focolare, come eri
una sera di Dicembre a predire
le avventure dei figli
dai capricci che facevamo:
"Tu pure non farai bene" dicevi
vedendomi in bocca una mossa
che forse era stata anche tua
che l'avevi da quand'eri ragazzo.

(1952)

Father mine

Father mine who are in the fire
swarming on the hearth, as you were
one December evening when you predicted
your sons' futures
from our temperaments:
"You won't do well, that's for sure" you said
noticing a twist to my mouth
that was perhaps like yours
when you were young.

Palazzo reale di Portici

Dai grandi archi della Reggia
il mare è il primo a farsi vedere
bianco sotto le luci nere
delle nubi lasciate dal giorno.
Verso le grandi chiome dei pini
spunta una Napoli corallina
con le sue luci di palco.
Degli amici vicini e lontani
cade il ricordo, come cade la ghianda
dalla nuvolaglia dei lecci.

(1952)

Royal Palace at Portici

From the great arches of the Royal Palace
the sea is the first thing to appear
white under the black lights
of the clouds left from the day.
Against the tall foliage of pines
a coral Naples stands out
with its stagelights.
The memory of friends near and far
falls, as the acorn falls
from the cloudmass of the holm-oaks.

I pastori di Calabria

Alle case arse di Paola sul mare
tra i fichi contorti e le fiumare,
che calano dai letti i sassi morti,
i Calabresi scesi dalla Sila
vanno a affondare le mazze nell'acqua:
non è più la pila per le vacche, è il mare.

(1952)

The shepherds of Calabria

When they have come down from the Sila
to the scorched houses of Paola on the sea
among the gnarled fig trees and the streams
that tear dead boulders from their beds,
the Calabrians go to plunge their walking-staffs in the water:
no longer the cows' watering-trough but the sea.

Additional poems

These poems were not in the
original posthumous volume *È fatto giorno*.
They were in the possession of Carlo Levi
who was planning to publish them
but was prevented by his death.

L'Adige scroscia

Hai visto per le montagne trentine
gioca il vento le sue rapine
sugli uomini che parlano quieti
sotto i campanili.
Le strade sono lacere ferite.
L'Adige scroscia qua dalla barriera.
Questa è la terra straniera
dei monaci bianchi
che sono i monti di neve.
Qui può stancarsi la melanconia
perché mi sono disperso e il mio grido
s'agghiaccia nella gabbia della funivia.

(Trento-Bolzano, dicembre 1942)

The Adige thunders

You've seen the wind through the mountains
around Trent
robbing the men who talk quietly
under the bell-towers.
The streets are ripped wounds.
The Adige thunders this side of the barrier.
This is the foreign land
of the snow-capped mountains,
those white monks.
Here melancholy grows tired
because I'm lost and my shout
freezes in the cage of the cable car.

(Trento-Bolzano, December 1942)

La nebbia veloce

La nebbia veloce ci recinge
non basta silenzio di tomba
per il freddo addio che mi dai.
Per te si è vendicata la figliuola
che nel dolce paese abbandonai.
Non si dissolve questa nebbia
che intorno ci creiamo. E le distanze
le più certe appagano la mia
ansia che pure qualcuno
mi viene dietro nella nebbia
col lume acceso d'una finestra.

The quick fog

Quick fog presses in on us.
The silence of the grave is not enough
for the cold goodbye you give me.
The girl I abandoned in my dear village
is revenged through you.
This fog we create around us
doesn't dissolve. And the surest distances
calm my anxiety
for fear someone is following me
in the fog by the light
from a lit window.

Mare di nebbia

Che giro di valzer
delle quercie nelle lastre:
hai visto il mare
sotto Ferrandina?
E' la nebbia della mattina
e le montagne più alte coi paesi
che penisole snelle!
Si frange ai bordi
contro i pini d'una villa
respirano gli ulivi
è vero che il mare
illumina la terra.
Schienali di montagne
toccate dal lieve sole d'inverno
si vede la pozza lucente
che diventa il nostro fiume.

Sea of mist

What waltzing turns
the oaks make over the paving-stones!
Have you seen the sea
below Ferrandina?
It's the morning mist
and the highest mountains with their villages—
what slim peninsulas!
Its edges shatter
against a villa's pines.
The olive trees breathe.
It's true: the sea
illuminates the land.
Backbones of mountains
touched by the light winter sun.
You can see the shining pool
that becomes our stream.

Viaggi

Pochi sbancano le ombre della notte;
andiamo nelle corriere
incontro allo spazzino dei paesi
che tiene le due scope
infilate alle spalle.
Nel crepuscolo mi stringe
un vicino orizzonte.
Una nebbia azzurra
nasce dalla terra.
E passa davanti alle lastre
io lo vedo così buono il mio nemico,
ritagliato con le forbici
nei suoi lustri contorni.

Few figures dispel night's shadows.
Let's take the bus
to meet the village street-sweeper
with his two brooms
hung on his back.
At dusk a nearby
horizon presses in on me.
A blue mist
rises from the ground.
I see my enemy pass tamely
in front of the windows,
a shiny
scissored silhouette.

Liberate, uomini, l'ergastolano

Chiuso nel cerchio delle mani
protese a un segno di liberazione,
mentre insiste questa pioggia
che porta nella stanza tanta luce
quanta basta alle tiepide cappelle,
han bussato alla tua porta nel silenzio
i contadini laceri del Sud,
i calzolai tisici dipinti
come l'acqua sporca della suola.
E sul libro le parole
riacquistano il calore della fiamma.

L'ora dei falchi solitari
induce al refrigerio
dell'ombra delle acacie.
Le voci sono le maledizioni
dei mietitori contro il sole:
non è tempo che la tua mano inerte
tracci motti sibillini
sull'arena accaldata.
Hai tu l'ergastolano nel tuo cuore
appeso alle sue sbarre,
così solo come sei.
I mietitori si son dati
convegno questa sera
a batter pugni sulle panche.
Essi sanno la mano sulla spalla
del datore di lavoro.
E sento che t'insorge la preghiera
tra le loro canzoni e le bestemmie:
Liberate, uomini, l'ergastolano.

(Napoli, giugno 1945)

Men, set the prisoner free

Closed in the circle of hands
stretched toward a sign of freedom,
while this rain persists,
bringing into the room all the light
that's needed for the lukewarm chapels,
they knocked at your door in silence,
the ragged peasants of the South,
the tubercular shoemakers stained like the water
in which they soak the soles.
And in the book the words
again take on the flame's heat.

The hour of the solitary hawks
tempts us to the coolness
of the acacias' shade.
The voices are those of mowers
cursing the sun:
it's not time for your inert hand
to trace sybilline words
on the warm sand.
In your heart you hold the prisoner
clinging to his bars,
and so alone—like you.

The mowers
are meeting tonight
to pound their fists on the benches.
They know the tap on the shoulder
from the boss who doles out jobs.
Between their songs and curses
I hear the prayer rising:
Men, set the prisoner free.

(Naples, June 1945)

Vico Tapera

Vico Tapera, uomini affaticati,
brache e collari lucidi
del sudore degli anni,
ecco nel tuo ventre i muli impazziscono
sotto il taglio del sole che ti assale . . .
Ma ancora si ravviva la tua sera.
Quella tarda tua sera
sospesa al sorgere della luna,
nella sua stalla giaceva
un giallo zappatore che moriva,
e noi sentimmo parlottare,
e il mulo muoveva l'orecchio,
e i cani sfiniti in lamentela,
e una donna si strappava i capelli,
Vico Tapera abbandonato
con mezza porta a battere col vento.

Vico Tapera

Vico Tapera, men, dead-tired,
collars and pants shiny
with the sweat of years,
look—in your gut the mules go mad
under the slash of the attacking sun.
But in the evening you come alive again.
In that late evening of yours
suspended from the moon's surge,
a yellow-skinned hoer
lay dying in his stall.
We heard the muttering;
the mule twitched an ear,
the tired dogs howled,
and a woman tore her hair.
Deserted Vico Tapera,
with your half-doors banging in the wind.

I manifesti

Continuerò a lanciare
dall'abbaino alto nel deserto
degli embrici dei tetti
i miei fogli manifesti
alla rapina funesta
dell'immondizzaio.
Dove i cafoni mangiano la polvere
ma temono per gli occhi, di non vedere
ai confini delle porte
si fermeranno quei pezzi di carta
buoni da calpestare.
Ma se c'è vento che turbinio!

(1946)

Manifestos

I'll go on hurling
my paper manifestos
from the high attic-window in the desert
of roof-tiles
for the deadly pillaging
of the trash-collector.
Where peasants eat dust
but fear for their eyes.
Those bits of paper good only for trampling
will stop
just outside the doors.
But if there's wind—what a whirling!

Invettiva alla solitudine

E questo tuono di ferraglie sul Rettifilo
oh come ripete il verso costante, lo stesso
del vallone squarciato del paese,
ove ai piedi delle case il Milo,
torrente dell'inverno e dell'estate,
annacqua gli orti pingui sulle pietre.
Lì vola oggigiorno lo stuolo dei torchiari
(che cercano assetati
disdetti dalla torre normanna
colombi del ritiro sulla rupe?)
e di notte il lamento dell'assiolo
strazia davanti le porte
il sonno dei frantoiani.

Quale smania ti prende, amico all'uomo,
di scendere al tuono sul Rettifilo!
Lungo tutte le rotaie della terra
sigarettaie come queste di Napoli
ed anime difformi da noi
abbattute alla maceria della strada?
Nemmeno il sole più ci scuote,
il sole che viene dal mare.
O il disastro o la furia o la morte,
la morte che già vive in mezzo a noi.
E pittori e cantanti e poeti,
animali da serraglio.
Ma l'assiolo che strazia e il Milo bianco.
E il cieco di Piazza Miraglia che suona

Invective against solitude

This thunder of trams clattering on the Rettifilo—
how it repeats the constant verse, the same
as the gashed valley of the village,
where at the houses' feet the Milo,
winter and summer stream,
waters fat vegetable gardens on the stones.
The flock of *torchiari* flies there still these days.
(What are the thirsty ones seeking,
expelled from their Norman tower
like doves from a cliff refuge?)
At night, outside the doors,
the horned owl's lament
torments the olive-crushers' sleep.

What a crazy impulse moves you, man's friend,
to descend when it thunders on the Rettifilo!
Along all earth's tracks
are there cigarette vendors like the ones in Naples
and souls different from us,
struck down on the road's rubble?
Not even the sun can shake us any more,
the sun that comes from the sea,
nor can disaster, fury, death,
death that already lives among us.
And painters, singers, poets:
caged animals.
Still the heart-rending horned owl, the white Milo,
and the blind musician in Piazza Miraglia who plays

al fresco di mattina ai marciapiedi
vederlo che ci appare un Cristo vivo
disceso nell'inferno
il giorno che Gli strappano i veli nelle Chiese.

(Napoli, giugno 1947)

on the sidewalks in the coolness of early morning:
oh, to see him appear to us like a living Christ
descended into hell
the day they tear His veils off in the churches.

Quaremma, la vedova pazza
era la pupa col vecchio grembiale
volteggiava al turbine di febbraio
penzoloni da una fune sulla strada.
Bersaglio di terribili fanciulli
periti nelle gare a sassaiola:
sfogavano l'ira dei padri neri
per tutte le piogge mancate
e i grani venivano su magri.
Coperto d'uno dei nostri mantelli
anche il cielo era lontano da noi
e avrei voluto vedere
quale parte recitava.
Dietro il recinto dei monti
i cavalloni squarciavano nitriti
in faccia sul mar Ionio
e pure il sole ci cacciava agli occhi
un'ombra vacillante di candela.
Intanto non puoi chiudere la bocca
ai divini germogli della terra.
Fuori il vento che frana sulle porte
sta a suonare la marcia del ribelle,
ma i mandorli sbocciati
picchettano i seminati,
i cavalieri bianchi della morte.

(11 febbraio 1948)

Lent '48

Quaremma, the crazy widow,
was the effigy with the old pinafore
that spun in the February gale,
dangling from a rope above the street.
Target of terrible boys
skilled in stone-throwing contests:
they vented their fathers' dark anger
for all the rains that never fell,
the wheat that came up spindly.

Covered by one of our capes
even the sky was a long way off;
I would have liked to see
what part it was playing.
Behind the mountains' limit,
on the Ionian sea the waves' white horses
whinnied in our faces
and the sun drove into our eyes
a candle's flickering shadow.

Meanwhile you cannot keep earth's
divine buds from opening.
Outside, the wind that landslides onto doors
plays the rebel's march,
but flowering almond trees
stipple the sown fields,
white knights of death.

Non tornano gli agnelli
per una fanciulla scomparsa

Noi ci teniamo lontani
come due lampioni nella nebbia
chiusi nel chiarore d'un metro
su due panchine nell'aria di vetro.
E' intorno lo stesso denso splendore
ma chiunque ha paura
di somigliarsi nell'ansia di amore.
Anche i nostri pastori
guardano inebetiti
gli agnelli che non tornano
che sono fuggiti.
Io non amo le statue nel giardino
ma una quercia che può sempre tremare
e uno le può parlare
con la bocca profumata di vino.
Attorno a te la nebbia è così forte
non ti si vede il soprabito stinto
che un giorno avevi e com'eri contenta
ferma statua che ha l'occhio della morte.
Deluso che la tua vita era calda
io me ne andrò bruciando mozziconi
non voglio farmi spegnere dall'alba
come questi lampioni.

(giugno 1948)

The lambs do not come back
for a dead girl

We stand apart
like two lamp-posts in the fog
shut into a small patch of brightness
on two benches in the brittle air.
Around us the same dense splendor
but anyone—no matter who—is afraid
of seeming alike in the anxiety of love.

Our shepherds, too,
regard with stupefaction
the lambs that have run away
and don't come back.
It's not the statues in the garden that I love
but an oak that just might tremble;
one can talk to it
with a mouth perfumed by wine.
The fog's so thick around you
the faded coat you once had
is invisible; how pleased you were with it,
motionless statue with the eyes of death.
Frustrated because your life was warm
I'll leave, burning cigarette-butts.
I don't want dawn to extinguish me
like these street-lights.

Montescaglioso

alla vedova di Giuseppe Novello

Mai perso bene questo sole e l'acqua,
ma quando la tempesta vendemmia le vigne
i cani si fanno irosi, addentano,
impazziscono le donne distese nei letti,
allora l'ultimo cerchio che fa l'acqua è nostro,
c'è sempre chi getta la pietra nel pozzo.

Tutte queste foglie ch'erano verdi:
si fa sentire il vento delle foglie che si perdono
fondando i solchi a nuovo nella terra macinata.
Ogni solco ha un nome, vi è una foglia perenne
che rimonta sui rami di notte a primavera
a fare il giorno nuovo.
E' caduto Novello sulla strada all'alba,
a quel punto si domina la campagna,
a quell'ora si è padroni del tempo che viene,
il mondo è vicino da Chicago a qui
sulla montagna scagliosa che pare una prua,
una vecchia prua emersa
che ha lungamente sfaldato le onde.

Cammina il paese tra le nubi, cammina
sulla strada dove un uomo si è piantato al timone,
all'alba quando rimonta sui rami
la foglia perenne in primavera.

Montescaglioso

for the widow of Giuseppe Novello

Never well lost this sun and water,
but when a storm harvests the vines
the dogs grow ugly, and bite.
The women go mad, stretched out in bed.
Then the last circle water makes is ours;
there's always someone who throws a stone into the well.

All these once-green leaves:
you can hear the wind of lost leaves
sinking furrows again in the crushed earth.
Every furrow has a name. There's a perennial leaf
that climbs back onto the bough on a spring night
to make day new.
Novello fell on the road at dawn;
at that point you look out over the whole countryside,
at that hour you're master of the time to come.
The world is near, from Chicago to here
on the scaly mountain that looks like a prow—
an old prow that has risen
and flaked the waves a long time.

The village walks among clouds, walks
along the road where a man has set himself at the helm
at dawn when the perennial leaf
climbs back onto the bough in spring.

America scordarola

Per te che te ne vai
senza nemmeno dirci addio
dove ti piangi la morte vicina
(perché ti stanca tapparti in cantina
qui nei giorni grigi di pioggia)
noi vedremo giocare il tuo bambino
alla lippa attorno alle caldaie
che accolgono l'acqua piovana.
Ma tu la mano non gli tenderai,
se gl'infiggono i chiodi i piedi scalzi,
con una busta di pesos!

Torna nuovo qui da noi:
ti laverai la faccia nel mattino,
tu ti ricredi vivo, ma smarrisci
a noi piano nell'ombra del passante
che svolta al grappolo di case,
lì gli autobus sono seri e fatali.
Torna, è tempo che assaggi
molliche di focaccia,
e l'odore dei forni
come te lo manderemo?
Scrivici, oscilla una corda
tra noi sopra il mare,
e tu la vuoi spezzare?
Ancora noi giuochiamo all'altalena.
ritorna alla tua pena di qui,
il bambino si fa grande
e i suoi occhi si cercano attorno.
In quanti ti daremo il benvenuto,
ti ritrovi in tuo figlio cresciuto:

For you who leave
without so much as a goodbye
where you weep at approaching death
(because you're tired of being cooped up in the wine-shop
here in the gray days of rain),
we'll see your little boy
play tip-cat round the tubs
that catch rainwater.
But you won't stretch a hand to him
with an envelope of *pesos*
if he gets nails stuck in his bare feet!

Come back fresh to us:
you'll wash your face in the morning.
You'll think yourself alive again, but you slowly
disappear in the shadow of a passerby
who turns at the cluster of houses.
There the buses are serious and deadly.
Come back; it's time for you to taste
flatbread crumbs
and how can we send you the ovens' smell?
Write to us: a cord vibrates
between us over the sea
and you, you want to snap it?
We still play on the swings.
Come back to your troubles here;
your boy is growing up,
his eyes search everywhere.
So many of us will welcome you,
you'll see yourself again in your grown son:

devi placare le sue ali goffe
come di una cetonia catturata
che vola legata al filo.
Egli porta già la testa
scontrosa nel mantello
e che sguardi ti comunica
sul ponte del fiume
illuso di atterrirti fin laggiù.

Ma papà l'americano non scrive più.

(1949)

you need to calm his clumsy wings
so like those of a captive beetle
that flies tied to a string.
Already he hides his sulky head
in his cape.
What dark looks he sends your way
from the bridge over the river
in the delusion that he'll terrify you over there.

But the American papa has stopped writing.

Conosco

Conosco tutte le mosse di mia madre,
del gatto sui tetti e nella casa,
la voce del vento che muove
il colombo di ferro al comignolo,
le piante che rinascono ogni primavera,
gli sposi e i giovani che sognano.
E voi, voi non avete altro da
inventare: occhiali per pararvi
dal sole, costumi per scoprire
un pezzo di carne alla volta.
Tra vento e gelate quest'anno vino poco . . .

I know

I know my mother's every movement,
every move the cat makes on roofs and in the house,
the wind's voice stirring
the iron dove on the chimney-top,
the plants reborn each spring,
the married couples and the young people with their dreams.
And you, you have nothing left
to discover: dark glasses to protect yourselves
from the sun, clothes that reveal
one piece of flesh at a time.
Between wind and icy cold, little wine this year . . .

NOTES

Capostorno: *"Capostorno"* is a chronic brain disease of cows, horses, sheep, and dogs, causing increased intra-cranial pressure and dizziness. *"Quote"* are plots of land allotted to the peasants under a land reform scheme. *"Quotisti"* are the recipients.

Black puddle: This poem, dated 1948, refers to the first general political postwar and post-fascist election which followed the 1946 referendum for a monarchy or a republic. The dazzling papers are posters. Scotellaro's Socialist party was badly defeated by the Christian Democrats, in support of whom the Catholic ("black") clergy mobilized.

I am a wood bird: A prisoner who escapes is known as an "uccel di bosco," a wood bird. Here we are probably dealing with an escape through an act of imagination.

There was America (author's note): "Today the paternal illusion that a place called America still exists is finished forever. And Venezuela, which is all we're left with, isn't worth a glass of water from the Basento."

The ninety-year-old Garibaldino: The Garibaldino is one of the famous soldiers known as "I Mille," "The Thousand," who followed Garibaldi into Sicily and fought with him there.

Supper: "Morra" is an old Italian game of chance in which two people lower their right fists at the same time, and quickly stick out some fingers. They shout out a number between one and ten. If the shouted number corresponds to the number of extended fingers (the closed fist counts as one), it is one point to the correct guesser.

Economics lessons: The person addressed is Manlio Rossi-Doria, a very important person in Scotellaro's life. He was a teacher of agrarian economics at Portici.

Psalm to the house and the emigrants: "Will they be able to grab the gold ring" refers to a game played on the holiday of the Protector, with a gold ring as the prize. Scotellaro says in a note that he

201

uses the metaphor to indicate the disproportionate odds between the danger of falling, and of winning the prize.

The shepherds of Calabria: The Sila is a mountainous area.

Vico Tapera: A "vico" is a lane.

Invective against solitude: "Rettifilo" is the popular name for the Via Roma in Naples. The word "torchiari" does not appear even in regional dictionaries. For an interpretation of this passage see Professor Della Terza's introductory remarks. "The day they tear his veils off in the churches": images of Christ are covered during Lent.

Books by Ruth Feldman and Brian Swann:
The Collected Poems of Lucio Piccolo
Selected Poetry of Andrea Zanzotto
Shema: Collected Poems of Primo Levi
The Dry Air of the Fire: Selected Poetry of Bartolo Cattafi
Italian Poetry Today: Currents and Trends
The Dawn Is Always New: Selected Poetry of Rocco Scotellaro

Other books by Ruth Feldman:

The Ambition of Ghosts

Other books by Brian Swann:

Selected Poems of Tudor Arghezi (with Michael Impey)
Primele Poeme/First Poems of Tristan Tzara (with Michael Impey)

The Whale's Scars	*Living Time*
The Runner	*The Four Seasons*
Roots	

The Lockert Library of Poetry in Translation

George Seferis: Collected Poems (1924-1955), translated, edited, and introduced by Edmund Keeley and Philip Sherrard

Collected Poems of Lucio Piccolo, translated and edited by Brian Swann and Ruth Feldman

C. P. Cavafy: Collected Poems, translated by Edmund Keeley and Philip Sherrard and edited by George Savidis

Benny Andersen: Selected Poems, translated by Alexander Taylor

Selected Poetry of Andrea Zanzotto, translated and edited by Ruth Feldman and Brian Swann

Poems of René Char, translated by Mary Ann Caws and Jonathan Griffin

Selected Poems of Tudor Arghezi, translated and edited by Michael Impey and Brian Swann

"The Survivor" and Other Poems, translated and edited by Robert Maguire and Magnus Krynski

"Harsh World" and Other Poems by Angel González, translated by Donald W. Walsh

Ritsos in Parentheses, translated and with an introduction by Edmund Keeley

Salamander: Selected Poems of Robert Marteau, translated by Anne Winters

Angelos Sikelianos: Selected Poems, translated by Edmund Keeley and Philip Sherrard

Dante's "Rime," translated by Patrick Diehl

The Dawn Is Always New: Selected Poetry of Rocco Scotellaro, translated by Ruth Feldman and Brian Swann

Library of Congress Cataloging in Publication Data

Scotellaro, Rocco, 1923-1953.
　The dawn is always new.

　(The Lockert library of poetry in translation)
　Selected from collections È fatto giorno and La
poesia di Scotellaro.
　Includes bibliographical references.
　I.　Feldman, Ruth.　　II.　Swann, Brian.
III.　Title.
PQ4841.C65A24　　　851'.914　　　79-3229
ISBN 0-691-06423-7
ISBN 0-691-01370-5 pbk.